SUMMERHILL DIARY

Pg 100   34
   108   112 ☆
    14

SUMMERHILL DIARY

by

BJARNE SEGEFJORD

Translated by
MAURICE MICHAEL

LONDON
VICTOR GOLLANCZ LTD
1970

© 1968, Hans Reitzels Forlag A/S, København
English translation © 1970, Victor Gollancz Ltd.

ISBN 0 575 00598 X

102729
LF
795
L692953
S413

PRINTED IN GREAT BRITAIN BY
NORTHUMBERLAND PRESS LIMITED
GATESHEAD

Friday, October 21

I bought a *New Statesman* at Liverpool Street station. I had two hours to wait for the train to Saxmundham, the nearest station to Leiston; I was on my way to visit A. S. Neill's school. But on a back page of the *New Statesman*, among the advertisements, was an invitation from the Summerhill Society to its members to go to Clarendon House, Hammersmith, on October 21 to celebrate Neill's eighty-third birthday. It was then the 20th.

I told myself to forget about the train I was supposed to be catching. So I took my luggage to a cheap hotel for the night.

I arrived at Clarendon House next day in plenty of time. People were setting up tables and chairs and putting out the prizes to be won in that evening's tombola. A man came up and greeted me. Was this where the birthday celebrations were to be held? Yes, it was, but the proceedings wouldn't start for another half hour. But wouldn't I come in? I paid the entrance money and the man offered me a beer. He was a former Summerhill pupil, he told me, but I was not to expect that everyone there that evening would be. Some had joined the Summerhill Society as sympathizers, others had married former pupils.

I steered the conversation round to my companion. He was a doctor and had left Summerhill twenty years before. He quite saw that I, as a foreign visitor, would want to ask questions and told me to go ahead. I asked the silliest one first: had he learned anything? He smiled: yes, of course, he had. He had perhaps been a bit late in starting on serious study, but once he had decided to be a doctor, what he learned had stuck. Also, I must remember that he hadn't taken his medical exams from Summerhill: he said that presumably to remove any possible doubt. But he had learned enough there to carry on from that point and become a doctor. Had he ever regretted having spent most of his schooldays at Summerhill? Definitely no. What had meant most to him there was the comradeship, he said, the autonomy, the fact that no one interfered in the children's own attitude to learning, or towards each other, or, much of the time, in their behaviour. But, he added, to give me as objective a picture as possible, if he had gone to an ordinary school he would have got his degree two years earlier. I wasn't to take that as a criticism of Summerhill. He had had a good time there and played a lot, which is not granted to all children.

We had drunk our beer. It was a few minutes to eight and the hall was filling up. He excused himself, but before he left me, he introduced me to a couple at a table further in the hall.

The husband had been at Summerhill, his wife had not. He was an engineer and travelled a lot for his firm on the Continent, especially in Holland and Scandinavia. Oh, yes, he knew Denmark—and Tivoli—well, and his wife had been with him on many of his trips. We got on well. When a foreigner has seen the lights of the Ferris-wheel and has enjoyed a cold beer in the Grotto among noisy and temporarily happy students, it can scarcely be otherwise.

He too was satisfied with Summerhill. This was almost suspicious. Was there, perhaps, a conspiracy, everyone sticking together to counter the criticisms of outsiders? When one has read and heard so much that is good about a place, it becomes almost a challenge to discover something to its disadvantage, to find the serpent there must be in that particular Eden. I looked round. The Summerhill Society, the engineer told me, had between 400 and 600 members; the numbers fluctuated between those two figures. Obviously, they would not all be there that evening, but already more than a hundred had arrived. I would not have the time or the energy to ask all of them the standard questions. So I was glad that I was going to have almost two months at the school itself. "Yes, many of the people here have been to Summerhill," the engineer said. "Would you say that a common feature is that they are satisfied with the time they spent there?" I asked. He nodded. "But I don't think it was all that ideal," he added. I pricked up my ears. Here, perhaps, was the clan's betrayer. I asked him to amplify his statement. "Well," he said, "now and then some poor little wretch has a bad time at the hands of the more robust pupils." That was nothing new. I had hoped for something sensational; this was an anticlimax. Neill had mentioned it in one of his books. Or maybe it was there to be read between the lines. Anyway, it was not surprising.

The hall was a buzz of reminiscence when the object of the celebrations arrived. He paused in the doorway, the height of which he all but filled, and struggled out of his overcoat. If age had permitted him to straighten up, his size would have been even more impressive. He peered at the lights. His cigarette was continually travelling up to his lips. Then he began going the long round. Obviously someone had told him about me before he got to my table, because he said: "Ah, you're the foreigner." To assist his memory, I referred to our exchange of letters, which he did not seem to remember. "Come tomorrow," he said, "at seven p.m. There's an evening meeting for the whole school."

Once having greeted everyone, he began the round again, now sitting down to have a chat and a drink at each table. It took him a good hour or more to complete the round and at the end he could still walk straight.

A microphone was then put up on the stage and the master of ceremonies said a few nice things about Neill, to which in all politeness the poor man had to reply. He spoke of his trust and belief in children, which made it all easy. He spoke of the tolerance that flourished at Summerhill and of how unthinkable it was that the school could produce a Hitler or even a lesser despot. So far, this was all a repetition of what he has written in his books. Then he went on:

"The school's finances are still far from good. We still get nothing from the State and not all children pay the full fees. That my book, *Summerhill*, became a best seller in the United States two years ago and thus provided a steady flow of dollars has been a help, and soon we shall have central heating everywhere. At the moment there are sixty-two pupils in all, of whom forty are Americans. They come to us and try to learn English. (Laughter) In a couple of months another book of mine will be published over there which we hope will earn us many more dollars.

"We get a lot of visitors, and that is a burden, as it always has been, but I don't mind. They all ask the same questions and are given the same answers. (Jubilant applause) I greatly appreciate these parties you give, and have greatly enjoyed this one. Thank you all!"

I pondered what he had said about the same questions and the same answers. It was inevitable, of course. Since the school was started in 1921, more and more people had been making the pilgrimage to it. Such a school inevitably arouses the same curiosity in a great many people, which must result in stereotyped questions. I had to accept the inevitable too; I could not reckon on being able to get away from the stereotyped. The question I was most anxious to ask, and which, among others, I was going to Leiston to have answered, was this: would an attempt to give young people of continuation school age the freedom of Summerhill, or even part of it, not be doomed to failure from the start?

Saturday, October 22

Because the train connections to Saxmundham are so bad, the Saturday evening meeting was already in progress when I arrived. The chairman was standing by the screened fireplace. Beside her sat the secretary, making notes in an exercise book. Elsewhere in the big hall various groups were standing, sitting, leaning or lying. The groups tended to be made up according to age and, perhaps, to interest in what was being discussed and decided. The eldest had taken up positions on the stairs leading to the floor above, the midde age group was more scattered, and the smallest sat in little clusters round the members of the staff or the visitors. Some were crawling about the floor and causing a disturbance, not as an act of protest but just because they found it too difficult to sit still. Neill was sitting in a comfortable chair beside a door. He had a child on either knee and attentively followed the proceedings, steadily puffing at his pipe. His wife sat beside him. At the moment I arrived the meeting was discussing some chewing-gum that had been stolen from one of the bigger boys. The one who had taken it owned up. Suddenly, one of the small fry on the floor went berserk, shouting and screeching and hitting out as if he were at war with the whole world. The chairman called him to order, but that did not help. Neill was obviously irritated by the interruption, and the meeting immediately voted that the boy should be turned out. When he would not go, one of the masters carried him out on to the portico, from where he thereafter watched the proceedings, dribbling spit through a hole in the glass in the door. Every now and again he tried to push the door open, but the master, who had his back to it, was too heavy to shift.

Discussion on the chewing-gum affair continued. The boy who had been robbed wanted his gum back, or at least some compensation for the loss. The meeting considered this demand justified. But the matter proved not altogether easy to settle. The boy who had been robbed was a foreigner and had bought the gum in his own country during the summer holidays: he was not satisfied with the offer of a similar quantity of English gum. The chairman, however, was quite up to the situation. He proposed that the boy be given compensation in cash, an arrangement which was accepted.

The secretary at once set about calculating the value of the gum at the current exchange rate. That was my first impression of the cosmopolitanism of the school.

Whilst all this was being discussed, there had been considerable unrest among the tinies on the floor. It was easy to see who was causing it: a healthy-looking little chap with black wiry hair. He was being rather aggressive, and calls to order were only briefly effective. Finally, Neill's wife, Ena, stood up, took the boy to her chair, and sat him on it in a way that, though kind, made it obvious that she meant business: he was not to disrupt the meeting. She herself stood beside the chair. Though a child's nature was accepted, at the same time a limit was set for its expression at the expense of others. As always, the art consists in knowing where to draw the dangerous line between freedom and indiscipline.

I stood in a corner observing Neill, who on only two or three occasions signalled that he wished to speak. This was the man who, ever since his first year as a village schoolmaster in Scotland, had been so excessively optimistic as to believe that children are rational beings, with an identity and integrity that must not be violated, and who, since 1921, had run his school on the principles of autonomy and parliamentary democracy. This was *his* school, a thing he has often gone into deeply in his books. His staff has to accept the rules he has made. Loyalty to his ideas is a prerequisite for getting on in that little community, and any who cannot see that, or who, perhaps, do not agree with Neill, cannot expect to last long.

Does he hire and fire his staff as he sees fit, arbitrarily? That is the impression his books give; yet it is not quite correct. The children have the right to bring up any subject, no matter what, at these meetings. This naturally includes matters concerning the qualifications, or lack of them, of the staff. After I had attended several of the "general" and "special" meetings, I realized that it is perfectly possible for a member of the staff to have his dealings with the children process of exterminating each other until stopped by the outside power of the grown-ups. This novel is an excellent picture of mankind's present situation and it forces the question: who is going to save mankind from exterminating itself? For the power to which mankind is subject is itself powerless.

Neill believed in self-government and democracy, because he had thought the right thoughts. Not democracy in the current concept of dictatorship of the majority; nor in the Quaker's definition of the word, which is that you discuss and go on discussing until everyone is agreed. Neill's democracy is, of course, based on decision by the majority, but it takes requisite heed of the needs of the minority. You will find examples of this in his books, so there is no need to explain it here. Nonetheless this form of democracy is not the truth about democracy and, personally, I have a feeling that Neill is far from satisfied with his democracy—or, to place the responsibility more equitably, the school's democracy. In his books, he sounds as though he is well satisfied with it, yet he is constantly quoting what Ibsen has Dr. Stockmann say in *An Enemy of the People*: "The majority is never right." This is assuredly true, because if the majority were right there would be no need for a minority to exist and our development would have halted thousands of years ago. However, minorities do exist and it is thanks to this that the outlook it not utterly hopeless. Which is why one must cherish the minorities in a healthy democracy. And it is this that Neill has been trying to do, though perhaps not always with an equal degree of success, for it takes a real man to keep a minority going with crumbs from the rich men's tables; for most people, and among them no doubt some of Summerhill's pupils, have a faulty concept of democracy. Democracy is very far from being a mere counting of heads.

Neill is a power-minded man who did not just admit democracy, because merely to admit is the approach of the spectator; he *ordered* democracy. It was something he required, a condition so that something positive might thrive, and that you could go in for if you wished or pass it by. Neill's case is the crux of the whole problem of power: democracy is impossible unless it is dictated. There is no case known to history of democracy coming from a social class or a large group of people. The demands for democracy have always been advanced by just a few individuals speaking on behalf of a greater mass. And the same is true of dictatorship. It requires a so-called "great man" to bring about either democracy or dictatorship.

To me the expression "great man" brings an immediate association with Hitler; and indeed it is true that the "great men" mankind has produced down the ages have been either great spiritual leaders or the worst of scoundrels. We are all subject to ambivalence and it will always be man's task to try and distinguish the scoundrels from the positive spiritual leaders. Unfortunately, history is full of cases where he has failed to do so, but there is no need to despair—there are, and have been, plenty of bright spots. One must be quite clear on this point: Neill is a dictator, but very definitely one of those the world needs. This may sound as if I am equating the democrat and the dictator as far as the employment of power is concerned, but that is not so. Dictatorial power will always have a false aura, while democratic power is based on a sense of responsibility for the whole and an attempt to hand this on by educating both children and adults, so that they acquire the same sense of responsibility. Power cannot be effective without this positive element. There is one other essential difference between dictatorial power and democratic power, namely tolerance. It goes without saying that dictatorial power cannot possibly allow itself to make concessions to tolerance, while democratic power has to. It is thus more difficult to be democratic than despotic. Behind democracy lies a greater perception. This is recognized in the saying that democracy is something one has to fight for. Dictatorship is self-establishing, as we can see when we take a look at the institutions of mankind—places of employment, schools, nation-states.

Throughout the meeting Neill supervised absolutely everything, and when some of the smaller ones created their disturbance, he let his displeasure be seen. But he did not become angry; it almost seemed as if he could not be bothered to. Indolence in that respect is a very important attribute, which many people could well cultivate. It does not do to divide your wrath into too small portions. Better to let it gush forth at the right time. That makes it far more convincing and effective.

After the chewing-gum affair and a couple of other minor matters had been dealt with, no one having anything else to put forward, the meeting was declared closed. The larger children rushed out, yelling like Red Indians, while the youngest queued up peaceably to be given their weekly pocket money. Neill sat with a cash-box in his lap and gave each of them 10d. for every year of their age. That done, he walked down a corridor, followed by the visitors, to the school's dining-room which also does service as a class-room.

It was then the visitors' turn to hold a meeting. Neill carelessly flung his cap on to the nearest table, sat down, lit a cigarette, threw the match on to the floor and asked if there were any questions. The last of the visitors who came in failed to close the door. "Shut the door," Neill said. That's what you say when you want the door shut. It was too much bother to say "Might I ask you to shut the door" or anything more flowery. He could of course have added a "please", but as every Englishman says please with practically everything, without being any more polite by doing so, there was little point.

Somebody's hand went up. Neill nodded.

"Are there other schools in England or abroad run on the Summerhill principles?"

"No. It would not be correct to say that the idea has caught on. There are a couple that resemble this one slightly, but it is a difficult school to copy in detail. A Summerhill Society was set up in New York and this started a school reputedly based on our principles. But it isn't. There, if a child swears and the master hears it, the master will wash the child's mouth with soap and water. As you see, they have misunderstood a few things about us. Fortunately, that is the worst example I know of."

"How many of the school's former pupils become eminent in, for example, politics—become a statesman?"

"There's a tendency to regard politicians as the world's leading personalities. That's what you are getting at, I take it? But there I must disappoint you."

The answer was accompanied by a smile that could be interpreted as an apology, and this caused the questioner to stick to his point.

"But surely it is reasonable to assume that a child who is brought up free should be able to qualify to become a leading person in the world."

"Who really are the world's leading personalities? Not the politicians. Who do you think will remember President Johnson in two hundred years? I cannot possibly think of the top politicians as the world's leaders. For me the real leaders are people like Socrates, Aristotle, Kant, John Locke, Michelangelo, Sigmund Freud. It is because of their ideas that the world has advanced in wisdom. Leaders of states seldom have wisdom. But several of them certainly know how to hate. I am convinced that if L.B.J. had been at Summerhill for any length of time, he would never have become president of the United States; to achieve that powerful position you require no small amount of hypocrisy, and to stay in power you have to go on being a hypocrite. And if, despite having been at Summerhill, he had become president, I am almost certain that he would have acted differently over Vietnam. He created hatred and caused it to spread.

Such characteristics are not usually found in old Summerhill pupils. I am very pessimistic about the world situation. The people one looks upon as the world's leaders are consistently heading for catastrophe, creating limitless hatred. On the other hand, I am never a pessimist where children are concerned. They can be as impossible as you like when they come here. Their parents, schoolmasters and psychologists may have given them up. But I always say: wait and see. I have not yet been disappointed, as long as the children have been here long enough. But unfortunately there's nothing I can do about all this hate-filled world. No, Summerhill has not produced any statesmen, but a lot of happy people in various professions."

Things had now warmed up, and questions and answers darted from one subject to another. Another hand went up:

"You are quite an old man now, Mr. Neill. What's going to happen to the school when you die? Could anyone else run it like you?"

"That's a question I don't like, perhaps because I don't like to face up to certain facts. That's not because I am afraid of dying—I'm not in any way—but only that I'm so fond of life that I don't like to think of it ending. But the question needs an answer. I hope and believe that the school will be all right after my death. My wife, who is a good bit younger than I, will be able to carry it on with a couple of good masters. There's no reason to think the school will close the day I go. But as to whether anyone will be able to run it like me? Well, I don't think so. I don't say that out of arrogance, but from a conviction that the individual is unique. Obviously there will be people capable of doing something similar and undoubtedly good, but I don't think anyone could copy me exactly. My ideas have not caught on to the extent I would have liked, but in the course of a long life I have had the pleasure of observing progress in the teaching and upbringing of children. Progress is being made. It is sometimes well disguised and it is certainly slow."

After about an hour all the questions people wished to ask had been asked. When he saw that there were no more questions coming, Neill had something to say for which he apologized, but said that the children had wanted him to say it. At one of the meetings some time before, the children had hit upon the idea that they might as well get something out of all the visitors and so they were to be asked to pay five shillings each, which was to go towards the swimming pool that was being built. Everyone coughed up for this good cause. Neill ended by telling those who had to stay the night that there was room at the hotel.

Sunday, October 23

It is not often in life that one has plenty of time, but I have now. I have decided to go up to the school mainly in the afternoons, and to spend the mornings in my room in the hotel writing up my notes. Today being Sunday was perhaps not the best day to visit a school, but the pupils must be doing something. In the school I worked at, it was usual for a couple of the masters to join forces to get the pupils who were there on Sundays engaged in various activities. When I first went to the school yesterday evening it was pitch dark and I was shown the way from the bus station near the post office by a former mistress who also happened to be going there. So I was not sure of finding my way on my own now, and decided to go to the post office, where I hoped to find a map of the little town on the wall. I did: a well-drawn map of reasonable scale. I searched for Summerhill in that part of the map where I expected to find it. Every building of any size seemed to be there: a factory, the grammar school, the electricity works and yet another school, but Summerhill was not there. I peered at every square inch of the map until I could have said with Napoleon that I had the map in my head. This was to stand me in good stead, for Leiston is just big enough for it to be possible to lose your way there once. I was lucky enough to find the school without using that one chance.

The thud and thump of a ball being kicked came from the playing-field, where the bigger boys, a couple of girls and two of the masters were playing football. The two masters did not do much, nor were they treated with any special respect. There was one group of girls standing looking on, but they were not so interested as to be unable to play a few singing games in between while. No one noticed me. I said "good afternoon" but no one responded. Two of the girls smiled, almost as if they recognized me.

Football has never been a passionate interest of mine. I had gone up to the pitch, just to show myself. On my way from there to the school buildings I saw a couple of boys climbing trees. They were high up. Perhaps it was just as well their mothers did not know what they were doing at that moment. A little girl was sitting on the seat of a swing, sucking a lollipop. In front of the main building was a young man who was dividing his attention between an aged Austin that he was polishing with cotton waste, a man in a blue jersey, and a young woman who was shivering in what looked like a big bedroom rug. I said "good afternoon". They looked at me and the young man gave his wing mirror a polish.

Inside, there was a quiet and stillness that I, accustomed to noise and commotion when pupils' time is not occupied with lessons, found strange. I recognized the hall. I had been there the previous evening. I had it to myself now. In the farthest corner a sort of platform had been built under the ceiling. There was a heavy, roughly joinered ladder up to this, and a notice saying that two persons at the very most might be up there at the same time. In another corner was a door that led into the school library. There was a notice there too: "Sorry—no visitors." In a third corner were locked double doors. There was another door, also locked. A staircase led up to the part where the older children had their quarters. On the wall of the landing hung a notice: "No admittance except by invitation." If one had not known better, one might well have thought one was in an ordinary school, with forbidden areas and restrictions.

There were two noticeboards in the hall. These had notices from the school to visitors and from various committees to the pupils, as well as the school's self-governing body's laws and regulations. The notices to visitors explained that the school could not give accommodation to any visitor whatever. Visitors were also not to ask to be allowed to sleep on the floor. The school did not like having to say no to these requests, and so they were not to be made. Visitors spending the night there caused disruption. The whole thing was so worded as to give the impression that once it had been possible to spend the night at the school. Reading between the lines, it appeared that you could spend the night on the floor, as long as you did not ask permission to do so.

I made notes of some characteristic laws and remembering that these were made jointly by the pupils and grown-ups on a majority vote, it would appear that children are not as foolish and rough as many grown-ups like to make out.

1. Neill's permission is needed to saw large branches off trees.

2. Playing with water indoors is forbidden. (N.B., the prohibition applied only indoors. Outdoors you could make as much mess as you liked. Splashing water is one of the human rights of childhood.)

3. Smoking, playing, eating or drinking in the library are forbidden.

4. No one under 16 may smoke cigarettes. (Nothing was said about pipe-smoking or chewing tobacco. Presumably these were considered too unlikely.)

5. Alcoholic drinks are not allowed.

6. If you are going out for any length of time, you should tell one of the staff where you are going.

7. Hitch-hiking is not allowed.

8. No child may swim alone. There must always be someone with a knowledge of life-saving present.

9. No playing with fire (including fireworks) in any building.

10. No one under the age of 12 may have matches or a lighter in his possession.

11. Only those of 14 or over may light fires in grates or kindle live flames.

12. No throwing stones.

13. No sticks with nails in them.

14. Swords are to be inspected by the staff.

15. No one under 14 may possess a knife. Knives have to be inspected.

These regulations are convincing evidence that children have just as much sense as grown-ups. Grown-ups, of course, helped to draw up the laws, but it must not be forgotten that the children are in the majority. It can also be said that grown-ups are better able to argue their point of view—or should be; and that, of course, is quite true, as I had experienced at the meeting the previous evening. But there can be nothing wrong in that. Argument sharpens the pupils' ability to appreciate and decide—a thing that is very badly neglected in ordinary schools. The arguments of the older pupils were often convincing, and obviously there is nothing strange in the fact that they are much more interested in self-government than the small fry are. But the small ones are gradually trained in the art, parallel with their ability to express themselves in words.

As well as laws for the pupils, there were a few regulations for visitors. The latter were not allowed to give the children money, spirits or cigarettes. I was rather surprised by the mention of spirits: it could hardly be common for grown-ups to bring these for their children? Perhaps there had been a case once. Further, if a grown-up was taking a child out for a walk, the child must report the fact to one of the staff. This, of course, was just a re-statement of the law that children should report an intended absence of any length. Grown-ups were asked to see that the child was washed, tidy and in clean clothes. This might sound as if this was another school subservient to the dictatorship of "what other people think", but the explanation is to be sought in two factors. In the first place, grown-ups (mostly parents) like their offspring not to look like tramps when they are in the little town; that is to say, the rule was made out of consideration for what parents, or some parents, think. Secondly, Neill cannot want the school to get a bad reputation. And there is a financial aspect to this as well: a school with the reputation that its children are dirty, muddy and ragged is not likely to have so many pupils sent to it. At any rate there is no need to take a risk of this kind.

I did not see a soul while I was in the hall. The school appeared strangely deserted. I went outside to have a look round. It was clear that the regulations for visitors did not allow me to stick my nose into everything, so I contented myself with a reconnaissance of the outside.

Compared with the new central schools of Denmark, or even with my old and hopelessly antiquated council school as I remembered it, Summerhill appeared quite simply archaic. I mention this as a matter of record, and also because so many people are infatuated by all that is "modern". If the interior was like the exterior, many modern-minded parents would think twice about sending their children here. There were several buildings, some quite simply huts. Three classrooms in a row were like tool sheds. The handicraft room (I took a peep through the window) looked as if it had been a poultry house before the children took it over. The two railway coaches mentioned in the book, *Summerhill*, which have been joined together and made into living quarters, did not resemble railway coaches. You had to look carefully to discover what they were. At the end of a long barrack-like building was something between a greenhouse and an elongated bungalow. Curtains had been drawn across its large windows, but behind this screen was stir and bustle of younger children. This must have been the old infirmary, which is no longer in use as such because the health of the pupils is so good. It was built many years ago by the staff and visitors, after the children had given up the attempt to do it themselves, once they realized what they had let themselves in for by voting for the project.

Though the oldest of them all, the main building, was the most dignified, it, too, had known better days. Before it became a school it had been a rich man's home, surrounded by gardens and a park. Of the trees in the park only the largest and best for climbing remained; these were no doubt fully appreciated for the excitement and views they provided. The old elegant gardens and lawns were now nothing but holes, gravel, mud and straggly weeds, but these all meant something to the children—not least that part of the grounds where the big swimming pool was being built. A couple of girls and a boy were standing on the edge of a big hole staring down at the reinforced concrete. They told me that the swimming pool had been promised to be ready within a year. Furthermore, I was told that they were making it themselves, except for a few things for which professionals were used in the interests of safety. The main building itself must have been rather splendid in its day, but Neill maintained that the troops quartered in it during the last war had done more damage than twenty years' wear and tear by children. And I should think he was right.

Monday, October 24

It seems to be an unwritten law that Neill only gives attention to visitors on Saturdays, or so I gathered after exchanging a few words with a female member of the staff yesterday. I had asked if there was any chance of meeting Neill, but was told that he had gone to the sea with his family; but that I could ask him all my questions on Saturday. Well, there was nothing to be said to that, when one remembers what he had said about visitors in his speech of thanks at his birthday party.

Today I pottered about as I did yesterday, trying to appear as if I might decide to move in at any moment. No one except Neill spoke to me. On his way to an English lesson Neill told me that I was to look round as much as I wanted. No mention was made of the notices, which some people could easily interpret as signs of lack of hospitality. I got the impression that he was leaving it entirely to me how I played my cards. No guide-lines, just a hospitable remark. I thought it wisest, however, to respect the notices, mostly because I would myself not relish people barging their way into my house. I exchanged a couple of brief remarks with some of the pupils, so that they should not think I was deaf and dumb. But back in my hotel room I began to wonder which of the people I had spoken to today had been pupils and which had been staff. They were difficult to distinguish. The pretty fair-haired girl surely could not have been a pupil—and yet—I just couldn't make up my mind.

Tuesday, October 25

There had not yet been time for my letter giving my hotel address to reach home, so the first letter I got was addressed to the school and it was waiting for me when I arrived there today. A middle-aged man—he at least was definitely not a pupil—came up and asked me if I was me. His name was Harry and he taught handicrafts. Then to my surprise he began talking perfectly good Danish. He told me that he had worked at the school for twenty-two years with an interval of a couple of years in the 1950s when he had taught at a school for difficult children in Fredrikssund. I was given my letter and he went into his class-room.

I did not follow, but went into a small living- or sitting-room which, as far as I could see, was not forbidden to me, although I was not invited in. It was very lively in there. The children were aged between 6 and 7 and between 9 and 10. Obviously they were not having a lesson, but I could not manage to ask them why. But perhaps I could arrive at the reason by listening to what they were saying, in the odd moments when the all but constant uproar made it possible to hear anything at all. Two boys and two girls were dancing round, holding each other's hands and singing. Two girls were engaged in a battle royal, belabouring each other with slippers and anything else handy. They pulled each other's hair, as girls do, and yelled and screamed at each other, until one of them evidently had had enough and began to cry. Active hostilities were now discontinued in favour of abuse. When verbal escalation had reached its peak—that is to say, the limit of the combatants' vocabulary—hostilities were broken off and replaced by peaceful play.

The whole thing was disconcertingly like today's diplomacy, or lack of it. It made me think of the concepts of aggression and pacifism. From my theoretical knowledge of the school I gathered that the children remained unaffected by this sort of thing, and the episode was itself evidence of that. A so-called house-mother with a bundle of washing under her arm had stuck her head in at one point, but she must have come to the conclusion that neither of the two contestants was going to take harm, for after watching them for a while she had gone away. I took that as a sign that natural aggression should be allowed to work itself out, as long as there is no danger involved. On a world scale this is the role that UNO's peace-preserving forces ought to play. And I most definitely sympathize with both the house-mother and the peace-preserving forces.

Even so, I cannot help thinking that it is impossible not to influence children—and, for that matter, grown-ups too.

Any attitude must inevitably exert an influence: it is not only what we say that has an effect, but to a considerable degree what we omit to say. I mention this as an attempt to make a hole in Neill's assertion that he does not influence the children in any way at all. I do not believe it, and I would not like others to do so. For example, I consider the "objective" teaching of history, which many pedagogues laud, to be utterly uninteresting. A teacher can be objective, and thus boring, because he is in no way involved in his subject, but that is not a thing he can choose: one is what one is. And why should there be anything suspect in subjective instruction? All children and most adults are subjective, so why should one try to avoid influencing them? Of course, there are various kinds of unfortunate influence, but I would prefer to risk them than to be bored to death in the stagnation of objectivity. And it is possible to be both factual and subjective.

At Summerhill it must be quite impossible to avoid being influenced by that somewhat vague quality, the spirit of the school, which can be summed up more or less as follows:

The children themselves decide whether or not they will attend classes. Each child is free to choose how it will develop, in accordance with its ability and temperament, both emotionally and intellectually.

The grown-ups are on the children's side; that is to say, they try to protect them against authorities that seek to drive them or direct them into definite paths. The grown-ups are the guardians of the children's integrity.

No form of punishment is inflicted by the masters or mistresses or others of the staff. Crises of discipline are unknown, because the teachers have no dignity to preserve and because a child that cannot be in a class-room without disturbing the others is turned out at once.

The school's outlook being essentially pacifist, it could be imagined that its influence would result in a pacifist attitude in the children. And, indeed, I seemed to sense just this spirit after the first few days; but I must admit that I went there expecting to find it and in sympathy with it. Someone with a different preconceived attitude might on the same premises have arrived at the opposite conclusion.

The room I was in was battered to the point of being almost wrecked. Over by the window, a couple of the floor boards had been torn up, and the boards round the gap were wet and rotten. The paint was peeling off the window. Two of the panes were badly cracked and looked to be inviting a helpful soul to send a stone through them. The room was meagrely furnished. Along one wall, though with room enough to get behind it and hide, was an old wardrobe in which the children kept their dressing-up things. There were two armchairs: one of them had half the upholstery missing; the other could boast of two springs emerging from holes with frayed edges. Of the two I preferred the one with the missing upholstery and sat in that. I produced my tobacco and paper and began to roll a cigarette.

One or two of the children came across and chatted with me. I deliberately did not ask questions, but left that to them: where did I come from? how long was I staying? what was my name, etc.? When I had smoked half my cigarette, the largest of the children, a girl, offered to throw it away for me. I declined the offer, because there was a lot of the cigarette left. She stared at it, watching the glowing end eating its way down. A couple more times she offered to dispose of it. I still refused. At Summerhill there is nothing difficult about disposing of a fag-end. If there isn't an ashtray handy, you just tread it out on the floor. There is no parquet to be harmed. Neill and those of the staff who smoke strew ash, stubs and dead matches round them. It seems perfectly natural. No rule forbids it and none encourages it. The children too strew their things all over the floor: comics, cuttings, rubbish. The girl's concern for my cigarette was entirely self-interested. When I had smoked it down to my nails, I held it until it went out, the girl staring all the time.

Then I gave it to her and said: "Now you can throw it away for me." "Oh," she said, "there's no point now." She threw it away crossly, but the next moment she was laughing all over her face. I said: "You know perfectly well it's forbidden. You helped to make the rule." She made no bones about my being right, but, she said, she had wanted to see if I remembered.

It was meal time. The children queued up in front of the hatch in the kitchen wall. The day's dishes were written up on a blackboard. There were three dishes to choose from. Those who could not read had the chalk marks interpreted for them by those who could. Perhaps this itself might act as a spur and make some wish to learn to read?

"Are you coming again tomorrow?" some of those I had been talking to asked. I told them that I was. I might even come back for a bit that afternoon.

It was that afternoon that I met Lars.

The hall was deserted when I got back about two o'clock. I read through the latest items on the noticeboards and went over the rules and regulations so as to avoid breaking too many of them. One never knew, one might be fined at the Saturday assembly. As I stood there at the noticeboard I was aware that someone was behind me, looking at me. I turned and saw one of the bigger boys standing on the stairs. I asked him some commonplace question, just to prove my peaceful intentions. He flung out his arms in a gesture of regret and said in Norwegian that he could not speak English. I then told him in Danish that I could not speak Norwegian. He smiled. So he had understood.* It was an amusing version of Babel. "Anyway, I've seen you before—what do you think of the school?—you were here for the Saturday meeting," he said. I told him that from what I knew of the school and had so far seen of it, I liked it. "It's too old-fashioned," he said.

* Translator's note: Danish and Norwegian are very similar, especially when written. One hundred years ago they were regarded as one language.

"The school in Oslo was much more modern." I asked him if he meant the equipment of the form-rooms and dormitories etc. or the way the school functioned. "Everything's so old-fashioned and worn," he said. "It all looks horrid. But we aren't punished." He was eleven. His Christian name was Lars. When I asked if he liked being at the school, he gave a very evasive reply. I said: "But this is a free school. If you don't like being here, why don't you go back home?" "I want to be here," he replied in a very decided tone and changed the subject by asking if I would like him to show me the school. I accepted the offer, curious to see what he would show me. Having been invited by him, I was within the law.

We went outside. He said: "I'll show you an old motor-car and a big tree." The car was certainly old. Lars thought it was an old one of Neill's. It lay on its dented roof with two wheels in the air. It had been stripped of most of the contents of the saloon and under the bonnet. Wires poked out of holes and openings in utter confusion. I asked Lars if the parts had been removed so that they could play with them or to be used elsewhere. He thought the car had looked as it did now for as long as he had been at the school. And then he told me that he had been there only two months—since the end of the summer holidays. This explained why he knew no English.

"Let us go to the tree," he said. The tree was an oak that must have been at least five hundred years old. It stood more or less on its own and so had been able to grow both upwards and outwards. A rope hung from a thick branch high up almost to the ground. The first ten feet of the trunk had been cased in boards and provided with a few hand and foot holds. "You can see a long way from up there, I can tell you," Lars said. "Now I'll show you something." Laboriously he climbed into the tree. Obviously he had not been up it more than a few times. He climbed as far as the branch from which the rope hung and asked me to throw the end of the rope up to him. Soon he was swaying like a giant pendulum. "I didn't dare do this a fortnight ago," he announced. He repeated his little feat again and again, I helping by throwing the end of the rope up to him. Then I became hungry and told him that I was going to my hotel for a meal. Didn't I eat and live at the school, he asked. No, I said, because there's this and the other regulation against it, as he could read on the noticeboard. But, of course, Lars couldn't. He went with me to the gate out into the street. "Now I mustn't go any further," he said. "Will you be coming again tomorrow?" I promised him that I would.

Wednesday, October 26

Lars almost went for me today. "Why didn't you come this morning?" he asked. "I didn't promise that," I said; "I said that I would come today and it is only just afternoon." But Lars obviously felt slighted. We sauntered round for a bit; the old tree had lost some of its attraction for him today. So on again through the grounds, which were large enough to provide plenty of diversity: patches of grass, clumps of bushes, open stretches, long narrow paths twisting and muddy, and football pitches. Now and again Lars pointed to something and told me about it very briefly. He was anything but a thorough guide. I just looked about me and asked very few questions. At one point we found ourselves standing in the hall. I hoped that he would invite me up to his room, but he dragged me off to the little sitting-room where I had been before and there we sat, each in one of the battered arm-chairs. There was no one there but us.

Lars was not well. At least, that is what he thought, as he told me rather hesitantly. After he had made a few introductory remarks I realized that illness was to be our subject for the day. I could not help thinking of an acquaintance, now an old man, who, when I was a child, always regaled us over Sunday afternoon coffee with the latest deaths in the family and the latest accidents in Nørrebrogade. As we talked, it transpired that Lars was confusing the professions of teacher and doctor. I was a doctor being consulted. Later he had got so involved in his symptoms that it no longer mattered what I was, as long as I would listen to him.

Lars sometimes became giddy when he got out of bed in the morning, and so sometimes he stayed on in bed in order to postpone the unpleasantness of getting up. Sometimes he could have a giddy fit even after he had got up. He could not bear feeling giddy, because it always made him feel peculiar. I asked if he went to any lessons and he reeled off a number of subjects he was studying; in fact, just about every one in the timetable—it seemed an enormous number. Not knowing him properly, I did not know how much he was interested in or able to grasp. Nor did I have any knowledge of the school's diet sheet. Personally I am convinced that vitamin pills can cure many nervous troubles, in the same way as calcium tablets are excellent for people who think themselves cursed with insomnia. Most likely his nerves were playing tricks on him. I asked him if the children were given vitamin pills at any of the meal times. They were not. Perhaps it would have been better if I had been a doctor, then I could have made a thorough examination and set his mind at rest. I urged him to discuss the matter with Harry, the two being able to understand each other, more or less.

When I left the school that day, he accompanied me to the street, beyond which he was not allowed to go, and asked me if I was coming back the following day.

Friday, October 28

Today the tinies were having great fun in the hall. They had put up a horse there, making it as high as they could, and were playing all over it, ending in a great heap on the other side. They crawled under it, caught each other by the legs, and knocked the horse over several times. The noise was appalling, but no one came to quieten them. The form rooms were too far from the hall for any noise there to be disturbing, and elsewhere no one let himself be disturbed by such a thing as noise. So they could play games with noise unlimited.

The Summerhill timetable did not include gym. It would have been difficult anyway to find a room suitable for organized fun and games. But the sensible view is held that the children there get all the exercise they need, simply because they are allowed to play as they like. The extent of their activity is, indeed, astounding when you take into consideration the fact that lessons are voluntary. This might lead some people to expect that they would all just loaf about. Of course, some did loaf around, without the initiative, as far as I could see, to do anything; they were in a distinct minority and most of them were new to the school, having come after the summer holidays, as Lars had. The majority were usually occupied with something, whether it was lessons, digging holes, clambering about trees, making a cave, playing football, or whatever. They certainly got more exercise than most schoolchildren, who are tied to a desk for so and so many hours a day, with only a few hours for gym a week. The Summerhill children are in no danger of heart trouble or muscular atrophy.

In the long break between the second and third morning period each child was given a glass of milk, while the staff went to the common room for a cup of tea. As he passed me Harry said: "Come along with me, if you'd like, and we'll give you a cup." I needed no persuading.

The staff common room was no different from the rest of Summerhill, except that you could see it was not used by children. It was large and simply furnished. In the middle was one of those large oval tables that were modern in the days of my grandparents, and a number of chairs of different styles. There were a couple of glass-fronted bookcases and some musical instruments, the latter being the only things not visibly aged. There was a stove that had been converted to burn liquid fuel. The female members of the staff were huddled round it, alternately holding out and rubbing their hands.

Harry poured me a cup of tea, wiping up what he spilt with the sleeve of his jacket. Then he said: "Lars is saying something about vitamin pills. Have you been talking to him about it?" I explained what I had been telling Lars and repeated the essential facts of what Lars had told me. "Well, we know, of course, that he doesn't like being here. That's obvious," Oliver put in, "but I'm pretty sure that his tiredness and giddiness come from going to bed too late." I was told that Lars did not stick to the bedtime accepted by the majority in his age group. "I know there are a number of problems here," Harry said, "but we find it difficult—to understand what he says. He speaks so quickly and indistinctly. And I am the only one here who can understand anything of the language." I asked if Lars ever went to Harry's art room, if only to have a talk. Very seldom, Harry replied, and if he did, it was only to "spoil a piece of paper". "You understand him better," he went on; "couldn't you try to find out what's wrong and let me know?" I promised I would try, but I did not think it would be easy; nor, to be honest, was it a task I particularly liked. It is difficult to play the amateur psychologist, however honest one tries to be; even professionals make bloomers. I mentioned my reservations so that they should not expect too much. And it soon transpired that I had already made a bad start, for when Harry asked me if I had told Lars what I thought of Summerhill, and I replied that I had said I thought it a splendid school, Harry remarked: "Well, if you've already told him you like the place, you start off not seeing eye to eye. It would have helped him if he hadn't known what your opinion was—or better still, had thought that you didn't think much of the place either. But naturally it is no use trying to change your tune now. There's nothing to be done about it. You didn't of course know him when you first spoke with him."

Saturday, October 29

It's a week since I arrived. I feel quite at home, as one says when wishing to emphasize that something is no worse than at home. I can even, without straining the truth, say that I like being here. By and large I can come and go as I like. I say "by and large" because I have on some occasions felt less welcome than on others, but I may just be oversensitive. I have looked in on a couple of evenings, but there has been nothing in particular going on. The hall was empty. Now and again a lone child, or two or three together, drifted through and went outside, to return shortly afterwards and go upstairs to the dormitories. I have not yet been invited up there, or to any of the other "forbidden" areas; and perhaps I won't be.

The five-day week has been introduced at Summerhill. The five-day week has made more progress in England than in Denmark. As schools in Denmark are supposed to train children for business rather than life, it is not surprising that business sets the tone in this respect as well. Another reason for Saturday freedom—or whatever one should call it in this school where everything is so free anyway—is probably that Saturday is a general visiting day, like Sunday, and some parents have to come a long way to see their children. All the week I had been the only visitor, but on the Saturday morning I noticed some people who did not seem to be connected with any of the children. So no doubt there would be questions at the evening meeting with Neill. As well, a number of parents had already arrived. They were delighted to see their children and it looked as if their children were delighted to see them. It was raining, so we were all in the hall, and some parents were joining in the games—sometimes quite wild games. A group of more staid parents was chatting round a radiator, engaged in a lively discussion, very free and easy in tone: obviously, they knew each other.

Before I went back to the hotel, I stuck my head round the door to look at the 8-10 year olds, who were stoking away at their lunch—and not always observing conventional table manners. There was no grown-up to keep an eye on them. As on other days, they had had three dishes to choose from, but even when they had their favourite dishes, some of it was left on the plate. Here, too, eyes are often bigger than bellies. Also, there would be some who weren't particularly fond of any of the dishes and ate only to satisfy the worst of their hunger. At all events the cat sat there keeping watch over the rather appetizing-looking bucket for scraps, and gazing up in gratitude at any child who scraped a contribution off its plate into it. And what the cat could not deal with went to the quacking ducks and gobbling geese that padded about in the mud outside the kitchen windows. The animals at Summerhill have a functional purpose and are not there just to be picked up and petted.

While we were waiting for Neill's arrival, so that the Saturday evening parliament could begin, six-year-old Jeff went and sat in Neill's chair beside the door to the staff common room. From there he announced that he was the headmaster. He said this with a smile and in such a natural tone that everyone laughed. At that moment Neill came in. "I'm the school's new head," Jeff repeated. Neill bowed respectfully and Jeff guffawed. Neill poked Jeff with his finger and Jeff chortled. Then Neill said: "Might I be allowed to sit in my chair, then I could have the new head on my knee?" Jeff agreed to this. He snuggled up to Neill and was having a blissful time. The meeting began, but proceedings were soon interrupted by the tinies, who had gathered in a clump in the middle of the floor. Neill asked for quiet, but they would not remain quiet for longer than a moment. Some of the visitors smiled tolerantly. I wonder if they would have done so after forty years of it? That evening's chairman and Neill alternately called the tinies to order, but there was never quiet for more than an instant. In the end the chairman had to turn out the worst offenders. It would not be true to say that that deterred the others. They went on until they too were ejected. Meanwhile two or three of the grown-ups, much irritated, had left; they could stand no more. Neill was obviously irritated too, and no wonder, but at no point did he lose his temper. He sat there stoically puffing at his pipe, now and again taking it out of his mouth to ask the speakers to speak up or the tinies to shut up. It was a good example of the balancing trick that all education is.

The questions and discussion were prompted by complaints about those who tyrannized over others. Plenty of time was taken, so that all points of view could be heard. When one of the accused became too verbose in his own self-defence, and no doubt more or less consciously took liberties with the truth, he was greeted with whistles from those who thought they knew the truth. After the verdicts, the sentences: a warning, a serious warning, or a fine. Some of those fined complained bitterly of what a little way their pocket-money went. I noticed that it was mainly the oldest or older pupils who were hard up. And, another thing, the culprit seldom sulked. If you made a shindy, or contravened this regulation or that, when the time of reckoning came, you took it for what it was: the price you paid for your pleasure.

The last item on the agenda concerned the tinies who slept in the hut near Neill's own house. They were not complying with their bedtime. When the bedtime inspector came to chivvy them into bed, they crawled about the floor and played one trick after another on him. This had happened for several nights on end, and peace and quiet had not been established in their hut until about two o'clock. The matter was brought up by one of the house-mothers. She insisted that the relatively large amount of sickness there latterly was due to lack of sleep. And, naturally, the tinies were not feeling particularly bright during the day. Neill chewed thoughtfully on the mouthpiece of his pipe. One of the older pupils, with a sense for parliamentary propriety, pointed out that most of those whose conduct was being discussed had been turned out. He proposed that they should be re-admitted. So the disturbers of the peace came in again, after some time had been spent finding them. When they realized that it was they who were being discussed, they were quiet enough. What child does not stop playing when it hears its parents talking about it?

The assembly split into two pretty well equal factions, one advocating an earlier bedtime, the other considering restriction of the tinies' freedom best. The tinies did not speak: they sat wide-eyed, whispering a little to each other now and again, but otherwise just letting things happen. Nor did Neill say anything. People seemed to be expecting him to speak; several looked across at him. Finally, when the two sides were becoming heated, Neill took advantage of a pause to ask leave to speak. He said that the tinies obviously had a lot of fun at night, that this was a phase they would have to go through, and that it would soon right itself if people did not interfere. It was really their affair alone, since no dormitory was near to another. Neill's own suggestion was to let the tinies have their head and to turn a blind eye to their being a bit dull-witted during the day. After some argument it was agreed to reduce the three proposals to two and vote on them; Neill's proposal was one of the two, the other was for an earlier bedtime. It was further agreed that only those involved should vote. None of the tinies had so far spoken, but they voted. Their case was put for them by an older advocate who was better able to string words together. Neill's suggestion was adopted. The meeting was then pronounced closed.

The tinies, delighted at the thought of a night of fun, queued up in front of Neill to get their pocket-money. The older you were, the more you got; which is certainly in accordance with the realities of life: the older you are the more you need.

When each had received his due, Neill asked the visitors to follow him into the dining-room. People were eager to ask questions; scarcely had Neill asked if there were any questions before someone said:

"How can a school that does not receive a subsidy from the State manage? One hears so often that schools with subsidies are hard up."

"That's true. To be sure, we do not have much educational equipment here and what we have is far from being first class. But that is not an essential. I must admit that I have a daydream: of a rich man who has read my books and leaves the school a million. As you can see, that has not happened. If I had lots of money, I would build up a much better library. Many of the books we have were given us by kindly visitors, books they themselves had liked; there are many good ones among them, and bad ones too.

"A couple of years ago there was a programme about the school on British TV. I received a fee of £25 and the producer said that I was getting twenty-five minutes free advertising and new pupils would come flooding in. I did not receive one application as a result of that programme. But I had better answer the question more directly. Two years ago the school's finances were in a bad way. Quite simply, the school was on the verge of bankruptcy. Then my book, *Summerhill*, became a best-seller in the United States and enquiries from parents and pupils came pouring in. The many American pupils now at the school have meant a lot to its finances. It was both interesting and harrowing to receive letters from children who wrote that they hated the schools they were at. They hated their masters, and some hated their parents. Such letters always ended with a request that the writer might become a pupil at Summerhill. I got several hundred letters, and the school could have been filled to overflowing, but the number we can take is limited. At the moment we have sixty-two and that is as many as we can manage. When the flood of letters began we had to lower the age-ceiling for admissions to twelve. There is so much work with children above that age. It has always proved much more difficult to inculcate understanding of Summerhill's freedom-principle in the older children, for they have been subject to authority and power too long, and find it very difficult to change their attitude. A few can do so, but most cannot adapt themselves to the degree of liberty here, which previously they have not been able to imagine. As we do not keep pupils beyond the age of sixteen, this means that a child of, say, fourteen has only two years in which to acclimatize, and that is too little."

After this I felt I had to ask a question that had no doubt been asked a number of times before.

"In your book *Summerhill* you wrote that it is impossible to give a child over fourteen complete liberty—meaning liberty in the sense of Summerhill liberty—if he has not known it before. And your argument is that the child is then too old. Have you any other reasons?"

"Did I write that? I can't say I remember it, but it is fun to be reminded of something you once wrote but have forgotten. No, actually I haven't any other reasons. I can only refer you to the examples we have had. Children of, say, fifteen have behaved like babies when they came to Summerhill. They smash window-panes, destroy furniture, scratch on doors and walls, spoil mattresses, etc. All done deliberately. They are quite simply a burden on the others, a burden that preferably must not be accepted, so that others can enjoy the place. We cannot reform them in the short time they are here."

An arm went up elsewhere in the audience.

"How old should children be to be accepted at Summerhill?"

"Normally we do not take children under seven and none over twelve; at the moment there are only a few twelves who can come. In cases where there are special circumstances we can take them younger than seven. In the school's history we have had cases of children coming here at three; but these are real exceptions. Children benefit most from being with their parents during their first four years, though this depends of course on how they are being treated."

"When do the problems of children formed under compulsion and lack of liberty appear?"

"That varies enormously, but as a rule after about a week, when they have discovered that they are free to do a lot of things denied to them before. Then, when they discover that they are not punished, the problems arise. It is quite common for un-free children from autocratic homes not to show any particular behaviour difficulties at home. They have been broken in like horses. But as soon as they are living in freedom linked with a certain responsibility, the behavioural difficulties make their appearance. They find expression in many ways. Unfortunately, in many cases parents do not give us sufficient information. Perhaps their consciences are pricking them about the upbringing they have been giving—or omitting to give—their children. They send their children here to have them put right, and fail to tell us of their own mistakes."

"Don't the children sometimes feel the lack of a room where there is a little comfort and cosiness? The rooms I have seen here scarcely suggest either."

This last question was asked by a man who fairly obviously had come with a ready-made negative impression.

"There is, indeed, one place where the furniture isn't battered and where conditions are such as children have in most homes. This is just above the dining-room here. As a rule it is only the older children who use it. The smaller ones don't seem to be interested in being there. They keep to their own section. The slightly older ones, they like to decorate their dormitories with drawings, paper garlands, and paintings made directly on the walls. No, we don't feel in any way that they lack places where they can feel cosy."

"In teaching foreign languages is weight attached to learning grammar?"

"That depends on the child. If a child needs and is interested in learning the grammar of a foreign language, that will be taught. We have one child whose future career requires him to know something of German grammar. One of the staff gives him private lessons. But the main thing with all languages is to be able to speak them, and next to be able to write them. Some years ago we had a Danish girl here who knew no English when she came. At the end of a month she was talking with the others quite without difficulty and by the time she left she had a perfect mastery of the language. She continued her schooling at a Danish school and when I was in Copenhagen I met her and said I supposed she was the best at English in her class. She told me that she got the worst marks in the class for English, because she did not know the grammar."

While Neill was replying to the last question, he kept his eyes on me, as if expecting a reaction from me as a sort of representative of Danish schoolmasters, so I did give tongue, saying that probably the girl's teacher dared not talk English because of lack of confidence.

"That's your answer, not mine," Neill said. "But I think I agree with you. Far too many teachers of foreign languages do not have sufficient mastery of the language they are teaching to be able to converse in it with their pupils. Or rather, they believe they don't, and that to all intents and purposes is the same thing. Therefore they are uncertain and afraid of a pupil catching them out in a mistake, so they prefer to centre their teaching on grammar, in which it is much easier to be sovereign. Here a schoolmaster who does not have complete mastery of a foreign language should nonetheless converse with his pupils as much as he can. After all, how many people really have perfect command of a foreign language? How many speak their own language impeccably?"

Towards the end of this question-time a dark-haired man with a crew cut had come in and taken a seat somewhat apart from the rest, where he sat making copious notes. When there were no more questions and the visitors were leaving, he spoke to me and we got talking together. He was an American and taught at a writers' school. Rather meanly, I imagined a place that promised your money back if you hadn't won a Nobel Prize for literature within thirty years; but he soon corrected that idea. As he pointed out, what the world perhaps has most need of is people who can communicate in writing, people who can write without necessarily being authors. He himself wrote articles, and he also tried his hand at poetry and short stories, but burdened only his desk-drawers with the latter. I decided that I liked the man, and we agreed to go to the hotel together for a beer. It was a Saturday evening and there were not many people in the hotel bar. A few sat round the fire roasting their feet, and some hardy customers were established in the corners. The American seemed restless. He kept repeating that he must have a talk with Neill. He had tried twice earlier that day, only to be told that there would be time for that in the evening. But there hadn't been. Now he intended to try again in the morning. I said I thought that would not be a good time, but the American insisted that it must be as soon as possible, because he had to return to the States in four days. He had not come all those thousands of miles just to pass the time of day with Neill. He had already wasted half a day without getting to grips with either the school, its head or its pupils. I told him of my own experience and recommended patience, to which he retorted that with two months at my disposal I could afford to be patient, and here of course he was right. "Shouldn't we go to the Engineer's Arms," he said. "That's where the staff go every Saturday evening." I asked how he knew that and he told me he had asked, and seemed to regard that as the obvious thing to have done. The staff had to go somewhere on Saturday evenings—they had to do something. He was certainly efficient, that American.

We walked the thirty yards along the street to the Engineers Arms and pushed the door open. The place was packed. With many "excuse me's" we elbowed our way to the bar and bought ourselves gins, which we watered down in the hope that they would last out a good long conversation. The Engineers Arms was obviously a working man's pub and also the haunt of the Summerhill staff. A couple of the staff had got themselves chairs, the others were standing up at the bar. The American spoke to them. His introductory remark was greeted with no more than a slight, rather casual nod. I could see that they wanted to be left in peace, not to be pestered by visitors when outside the school. The American was not so easy to put off. He proceeded to chat away about everything and nothing, in a very friendly and charming manner. The responses he received were, in effect, polite requests to shut up. In the end, whether because he felt defeated or because he had exhausted his arsenal of politeness, he gave in. We drank up and left.

On our way back he said: "That lot's not very talkative."

Sunday, October 30

I was at the school horribly early. I was standing in the hall at ten o'clock. Some people say that one's best sleep is had before twelve o'clock, and I agree, provided you make that twelve noon. However, I had arranged with the American to go there that morning. I thought that I might learn something from him. I met him in the hall. He had already been there an hour and was busy with a tape-recorder. The tinies were flocking round to say something into the microphone. We fooled away with it, as I imagine everyone does for the first few days they have one. The children thought it great fun to hear their own voices. It was evidently the American's tactics to make friends with the smallest first. That was not a bad method and perhaps the only one that will get you anywhere at Summerhill. It is not difficult to make friends with the very young ones. You only need to play with them. And if you play what they like, mostly romping, they will drain you of all your energy. They will clamber up you, hang on to your clothes, want to be swung round, and so on. One afternoon, a couple of days back, we had great fun scampering about the floor on all fours, pretending to be monkeys. Usually it is the visitor who collapses first, but when they are tired of playing you can have a pleasant chat with them. Their vocabulary is amazingly large, which is undoubtedly due in large measure to the fact that the older pupils pay much more attention to them than is usual in ordinary schools and often talk to them. And it is natural for the larger pupils to accept a visitor if he is getting on well with the younger ones. Thus you establish contact with the older children, whom pubescence naturally makes more introvert.

At one juncture the American disappeared up the stairs leading to the dormitories with a couple of the children. I did not know whether or not he had been invited. However, as no one had invited me, I elected to go back to the hotel, because the school now appeared as deserted as it had been on the previous Sunday.

I did not see the American again until late that afternoon, when he came to my room and asked if we might have dinner together downstairs. During dinner he told me what he had been doing. He had seen all the dormitories, the classrooms and the library. I could not compete with that and he reproached me for not getting myself invited, as was so easy to do. He had simply fished for an invitation until the children had invited him. Frankly, I did not like his way of doing things, and in fact, I later told him so, in response to a direct question. "You won't get anywhere if you're so modest and retiring," he said. I replied that I thought I would, having ten times as much time as he had. He admitted I had a point there, but was afraid that I could do with more initiative.

After being shown round everywhere, the American had arranged a sort of psychological test, still with the young ones, in the dining-room. He had it all on tape. He had got them worked up to the point of running about on top of the tables. As far as I knew this was not a thing they ever did. Even when things got a bit out of hand in the tinies' dining-room, I had not seen or heard anything of this kind. I wondered what Summerhill would have to say to this: it was not covered by any rule on the noticeboard. What to me seemed stranger still was that, after that, the American had—how I don't know—incited the children against each other, and got them to go for each other. Some had been reduced to tears. I thought this quite uncalled for and told him so. He shrugged that off. "But," he said, "I've noticed that the bigger ones don't think so much of me." So his next campaign was to be directed at the older children. Perhaps he could hire a bicycle from one of them. He wanted to see a bit of the country, now that he was in England. Also, he had to have his talk with Neill, which he had still not managed: Neill had been at the sea today. Yes, he had several things to attend to. I felt quite exhausted by his energy.

Monday, October 31

Lars had not been well for a couple of days, Harry told me at eleven o'clock tea in the staff common room today. But this time it was genuine. Lars had a cold. On other occasions when he spent a day or two, or even half a day in bed, he was just playing truant. He took to his bed out of sheer boredom. He did not appear to be interested in learning the language, for he never played with anyone and no one paid any attention to him. So why should not a hermit prefer the warmth of his own bed?

I did not in any circumstances want to go to Lars' room without his invitation—which Harry agreed was right—and so I had nothing to tell them about Lars' difficulties.

I saw very little of the American during the day. He was rushing round with a notebook and his tape-recorder, sometimes in the company of some of the smaller children (he seemed to have extended the range of his contacts), sometimes alone. In the evening we again had dinner together. He was able to announce that he had had his talk with Neill. Scarcely had they settled themselves over in Neill's house than Neill told him that the older children did not like him. The American was well aware of this, and his reaction was most positive: he wanted to work away at making friends with them—and to hire a bicycle. Not much else seems to have come out of the conversation. But the reason why the older children did not like him was divulged: they had been very irritated by the way he had behaved with the tinies in the dining-room.

The American asked me if I was not going to interview Neill. I replied that I had the impression that Neill was not very interested in talking to visitors except at the Saturday evening meetings. The poor man was eighty-three and must have discussed the same things with visitors for forty years; and even though he did not talk with everyone, the total of such conversations must be very considerable. To Neill I was just one of the thousands of schoolmasters and mistresses up and down the world who had become interested in his school. It was that that concerned them, not the man as such. If we were to talk, it could just as well be on his initiative as on mine. I was there to have a look at his school, not to add to the burden of his working day. It was a busy day, mainly taken up answering letters and talking with pupils. Apart from that he did a certain amount of teaching, only sixteen periods a week, all English. I felt that he had quite enough to attend to. Not only that but I had a feeling —based on no evidence, I may say—that Neill did not hold teachers in particularly high regard. Nor do I.

The American grinned slightly at this confession, a strange one to him, and then suggested that we go back to the school to have a look at the festivities, which a large poster on the noticeboard had been announcing for the last few days.

When we arrived, the carnival or whatever it was called was in full swing. Everyone was dressed up and some were quite unrecognizable. Some of the smaller girls were beautifully dressed, and kept going up to a mistress for repairs. It was obvious that the mistresses and house-mothers had helped the smallest. Lars was a cross between a ghost and a pirate, almost enveloped in a long garment, with a combined hat and mask. He had tattooed his manly chest in garish colours, which ran and mixed in the course of the evening and so he borrowed my ball-pen to redraw the outlines. I asked him if the costumes had been made specially for the occasion or were ones that were always there and available. There were some of each. A good number had been obtained from the dressing-up wardrobe in the living-room with the dilapidated armchairs, and some had been specially made. Lars also told me that there had been three or four such entertainments in the short time he had been at the school.

When the dancers were getting out of breath, the evening's master of ceremonies announced the performance of a sketch. An old sofa was dragged in from the library and shortly afterwards the first of the cast appeared, one of the bigger boys dressed as a nun. The next was a sailor. The content of the sketch was the sexual and the blasphemous: the sailor making approaches, the nun resisting staunchly. The sailor's victory followed, of course. At the back of the sofa, the nun removed her clothes, flinging them about the floor. She was well sheltered by the sofa, but did at least cause a sensation with the garments—and express the nun's feeling of having a right to a sex life. Everyone was amused. I thought of the sketches we performed at school: if I had suggested this one, I'm willing to bet it would not have been allowed.

After the sketch, dancing was resumed to gramophone music from the platform above our heads. The American spent most of the evening sitting with a sulky smaller boy on his lap. I wondered who was comforting whom. There was a distinct feeling that the American was *persona non grata*.

At one point in the proceedings Lars announced he could not be bothered with such nonsense any longer and left.

Tuesday, November 1

At seven this evening the American came and told me that there had been a special meeting over a case of theft that morning. Nothing much had been stolen, but as the thief has been caught red-handed they had elected to call a special meeting and this had been held in the long break. He asked why he had not seen me all day—I ought to have been at the special meeting. I reminded him that I still had another month there. Of course—whereas he had to go so soon.

It was obvious, though, that this was not really what he

had come to tell me. He had something else on his mind. He appeared to be irritated and shaken. "As you know," he said, "I had been intending to travel back on Thursday. But now I shall go tomorrow. This isn't much of a school to be at." What was wrong, I asked. Well, he had spent the whole day there, except for a couple of hours at Leiston Grammar School. And everything had been perfect until about an hour ago. Then, when he was crossing the hall, one of the older boys had accosted him and asked why he kept roaming about the place. He didn't belong there. The school was the pupils' home and he was a disturbing element; he should return to America. After a quarter of an hour's acrimonious argument, the two had parted without being any nearer agreement or understanding.

Now the American went on to say that tolerance could not be as important to the school as Neill made out. The daughters of two friends of his, after only a year at Summerhill, had acted as if he just did not exist when they were at home for the holidays and he was a guest in their homes. He thought that they might at least have pretended some degree of friendliness. Here he had seen the girls at school each day, but they had not come up to speak to him. He was amazed that he had not exchanged a single word with either of them. So was I, but then I did not know any of the details and refrained from asking. Perhaps the American was concealing something that would explain the girls' reserve.

He then invited me for a cup of coffee at the International Club. He also asked for some writing paper. Neill was to be written a letter! As we sat at our table, I drank my coffee without speaking, while he wrote away in righteous indignation, letting his coffee get cold. He wrote a first draft which he read out for my approval. I was far from agreeing with him, but preferred not to offer any criticisms, partly because I feel that everyone has a right to blow off steam and partly because I realized that my arguments would just be brushed aside by a man as angry as he was. Anyway, Neill could well stand being told "the truth"; he must have heard it often enough from those whose dignity had been hurt. The American wanted to hand the letter to Neill in person on Wednesday morning. He thought the result would be a special meeting, and he challenged Neill to read the letter aloud there for all to hear—pupils as well as staff. We arranged that I should be at the school at eleven o'clock, to attend the meeting, so that I could send him an account of what happened.

In his letter he described the hospitable reception he had received at Leiston Grammar School. There he had been invited to attend several classes. People there had paid attention to him. At Summerhill he had been cold-shouldered. His letter went on to deeper criticisms, claiming that Summerhill was a state within the state, an island without links with the mainland, where children were brought up to regard themselves as special beings outside the society of which they must inevitably become members and in which they would have to live when they left school. He seriously questioned the idea of bringing children up to be free, partly because he was afraid that this freedom would come to be felt as a prison in normal social life, and partly because he had been exposed to a degree of intolerance which he sharply condemned.

There are two things to be said about the American's subjective experience and reaction. His ego was wounded at the school. Previously he seemed to have encountered only courtesy, good manners—servility even—in a word, the façade which most of us have to present in everyday life. The children at Summerhill are not familiar with this façade. They are honest through and through, a fact that can sometimes shock those who are not prepared for it. The American's pleasant reception at the Grammar School may no doubt have stemmed from genuine interest in his visit, and genuine courtesy; but it is also conceivable that the interest and courtesy were shams. A great number of institutions, schools and businesses receive visits as a matter of course, and visitors are suitably received, that is to say with good manners and a show of interest even though neither need be genuine. There is less hypocrisy at Summerhill. If a visitor is not welcome, he will quickly become aware of the fact. And if he is welcome, he will be met with affection, interest and comradeship. The whole thing rests on whether the visitor has a positive or negative attitude to Summerhill's concept of liberty. His attitude cannot be concealed because the atmosphere at Summerhill is very sensitive.

When the American had made a fair copy of his letter and the strain of composition was over, he brightened and fetched two more cups of coffee. We remained for a long time in the International Club. Many of the foam-rubber cushions there had been slashed by vandals. We guessed that this must have been the work of brass-studded leather-jackets, and our assumption was confirmed when, towards closing time, one such studded individual in the farthest corner of the room cut a lump of rubber out of his seat, stuffed it down the front of his jacket and walked out. In his condition he could certainly cause Summerhill a lot of trouble.

Wednesday, November 2

If sins of omission do not count, one does not sin while one is asleep. Today, I got to the school a little past eleven and the special meeting was already in progress. To avoid disturbing the meeting I went and settled down in the little sitting-room. Later in the day I learned that I could perfectly well have gone into the meeting. They do not easily let themselves be disturbed, and anyway they had grown accustomed to my coming and going. As it was, I could not hear what was being said. But they talked for a long time; in fact, it was a few minutes after the next period should have begun before the meeting ended.

The first person I ran into after the meeting was Mitch. I asked him what they had had against the American. First, apparently, was the business in the dining-room with the tinies. Mitch continued: "He kept asking questions, yet the only thing he was interested in was facts and more facts. He showed no interest in us as people, he was not talking to our feelings, only to our intellects." This boy was only thirteen and his answer revealed no mean knowledge of people and their feelings. One could almost have thought he had read *The Little Prince*. At all events, we are concerned here with an aspect of upbringing in freedom to which Neill has drawn attention, namely that of making the subconscious conscious.

Later, I had a talk with Neill. He came up to me, holding the letter in his hand, and asked if I knew anything about it. I told him that I did, and what was written in it. He asked me across to his house. In the porch we ran into a big boy. Neill said: "Buzz off, we don't want visitors here." The boy grinned and held the door open for us with an exaggeratedly servile gesture.

We sat in two good firm armchairs and Neill got his pipe going. He even placed the match in an ashtray! Then he asked me to tell him about the American and how the letter came to be written, so I told Neill about the American's doings at the school and how the previous evening he had come to my room at the hotel after his talk with the boy in the hall. Neill puffed away, nodding every now and then. I ended with an account of our evening at the International Club. Neill said: "In this letter he says that I had invited him to come and visit the school and that he could not understand his being treated so inhospitably. But the fact is that the children here do not care for visitors. There are too many of them and they are a disrupting element. Normally they come on Saturday evenings to see the school's parliament, which to visitors is the most interesting thing about the school. But even that can be disturbing. Often matters are not brought up at these meetings because the children do not want them aired in front of strangers. That is why we have arranged for some matters to be dealt with at special morning meetings. But naturally I neither can nor would compel the children to be hospitable. They are, if they have reason to be so. I can only suggest that they should be because this can so easily have a financial effect on the school. Well—he's a writer, so now, I suppose, he'll go back and write a critical article in some magazine or other. There's nothing to be done."

I suggested that such criticisms could be counterbalanced if those who were satisfied also wrote about the school. He agreed; but, he remarked, the negative view always seems to have the greater effect. That, perhaps, is one of the reasons why I have not been content to write just an article. As forty of the school's sixty-two pupils came from America, Neill's fear of the effects there of hostile reports about the school was understandable. Presumably it was that fear and the topicality of the affair that caused the angry letter to be discussed at a meeting unattended by visitors.

"What especially turned the older children against the American were his strange experiments in the dining-room, and I told him so the following day, when some of the older pupils had told me about them," Neill said.

There were a number of books on the table in front of us. My eye had been caught by the title of one of them: *A Dominie's Log*, which was Neill's first book, published in 1915. I asked if I might borrow it. "By all means," Neill said, "but it isn't particularly good. Read it with reservations, because I did not know so much about psychology in those days. Fortunately it is out of print."

On our way back to the school, where Neill was to take

a class, we stopped for a chat with Ena in the kitchen. The talk was mainly about Lars. "The strange thing about him is," Ena said, "that he has been here nearly two months and still can't speak one word of English. At first we thought he had been sent here to learn the language, but we realize now that there must be greater problems where he's concerned, but we do not yet know what they are." Neill muttered something about home problems. This of course is becoming a stereotyped comment and regularly holds good. I cannot count the number of times it has been the cause—and the school has not been informed, not even in cases where the child has come from a social adviser or rehabilitation centre. Schools have to combat formidable secretiveness.

That afternoon I was invited into the "henhouse" to watch a crafts class, where the older pupils were working individually. One big boy was attacking a log that was going to be a sculpture; others were making tables and stools. The girls were making bookshelves; they had only just begun to take an interest in carpentry, and seemed to find it rather difficult. Peter had to show them how to cut wood, and how to hold a plane.

The work and products of this craftsroom were no different from what one is accustomed to from Danish schools. The youngest were making money-boxes (though what they, who were always broke, thought they were going to do with them, I don't know), swords and sabres, and some who were a bit older had done some excellent basket work. The instructor, Peter, was a newcomer, this being his first term, and he was not yet properly accustomed to Summerhill freedom of expression. He frankly admitted this, so he cannot have been altogether hopeless; but all the same I was surprised that he should require his pupils to make something to his specifications and instructions. He showed me an album of sketches and photographs of things his previous pupils in a state school had made; he wanted his Summerhill pupils to make the same sort of things. In the course of our conversation, however, it became obvious that they were not all that keen to do so, and would have preferred to make things they had thought of themselves. I asked if it was not all the same what they made, but he did not think so. He thought that they would do best to learn the basic principles of the craft, by making the sort of things he had in his album. I did not understand his argument and asked if it was not just as possible to learn the basic principles of carpentry making whatever one wanted. He did not think so, because that way there was always a danger that pupils would choose to make things they already knew how to make, and so would not learn anything new. This, at least, had been his experience at other schools; but he did add that his experience of Summerhill was still very slight.

I tried to delve a little deeper into the mentality of this man who seemed to be poised on a seesaw between compulsion and liberty. I asked him if it was not possible that the children were simply not interested in the basic elements of the craft, and came merely in order to have fun making something out of wood—and so, perhaps, would themselves discover the possibilities of the various tools under his guidance. Peter thought that this perhaps could be true, but, as he said: "It is difficult to give up a way of doing things to which one is accustomed and which you know leads to positive results and good craftmanship."

Neither of us was right or wrong—or rather, only the children themselves could pronounce us right—or the opposite. In the case of a child who really wanted to learn carpentry, Peter would be right; but if the child came because he was interested in playing with possibilities and giving expression by experimenting, then I would be right. All instructors should give careful consideration to their special subjects and ask themselves whether their methods and procedure are suited for each individual child's needs. Far too often promising starts based on real interest end in barren expertise, spoiled by teachers who long ago adopted a set procedure and closed their minds to further ideas.

At the end of the period, one of the boys asked if I would like to go and see how they lived. This was the first invitation I had had from a pupil, and naturally he did not have to repeat it. We walked along a muddy path to the two joined railway coaches which now housed the older boys. The coaches were connected by a living-room that had been constructed between them; and by giving it all a sloping roof, they had space for a fine lumber-room and hidey-hole above.

You entered straight into the living-room and this was dominated by a stove, with a stove-pipe standing like a pillar in the middle of the space. Very possibly its construction would not have satisfied Denmark's small-minded authorities, but it looked solid and seemed to function. Perhaps it did not leave enough ventilation for the occupants according to current ideas, but so far no one has perished in the building. The boys' rooms were in the actual coaches, which had a partition down the middle. Two shared each of the four compartments, which provided all the romance of railway travel. It was like stepping into a saloon. The original windows and ventilation arrangements had been retained and naturally nothing had been done to hide the curve of the roof. There was plenty of room for the beds to be placed at right angles, and for a couple of chairs, a table, and bookshelves on the wall. In one of the compartments there was even a plant in a pot. Colourful posters had been put up, but nowhere did I see a portrait of an idol. Perhaps free children do not need—or do not take pleasure in—the substitute authorities of the society of abundance?

When I had looked my fill, we went and sat in the living-room on an aged sofa that had been trampled by many children's feet. There were no more periods that day and several of the bigger boys joined us. In the course of conversation I said that I would like one day to get the oldest children together for a group interview. They thought this would be perfectly possible, but they wanted Neill and Ena to be there as well. Naturally I had no objection to that and we agreed to take the matter up again at Neill's next Thursday evening talk.

That evening and well into the night I read *A Dominie's Log*. Like Neill's other books, it was easy reading. I came to the conclusion that what he may have lacked in knowledge of psychology in those days, he had made up for, and more, with astounding intuition. Such things, of course, are difficult to distinguish. At all events, even today the book would, if not cause a furore, at least stir up Denmark's pedagogic duckpond.

Saturday, November 5

The last couple of days the children have been very preoccupied with Guy Fawkes' Day. They have piled up the materials for a great bonfire on the hockey pitch. And when I got to the school early this morning the cleaners were dragging the two dilapidated chairs from the living-room out into the yard; these too were destined for the flames that evening. The children had spent most of their money on fireworks. As English law forbids the sale of fireworks to small children, the older ones had done the purchasing. Now everyone had enough for a real balance of terror to be established. At my hotel people were also looking forward to the evening and, as a result, were talking more about the weather than ever—if that were possible. It had started raining during the night and was still doing so. The sky was the colour of liver paste and I think a North Sea fisherman would have prophesied a rainy day. All Suffolk's bonfires were going to be wet and smoky that evening, and people were correspondingly depressed. Inside an hour, while I was having breakfast, my attention was thrice drawn to the fact that it was raining. So at least it penetrated that I ought to wear my mackintosh. But I wondered, is it good that people here talk more about the weather, which they cannot alter, than about the important things they could do something about if they pulled themselves together?

Owing to the excitement of the children and their eagerness to get busy on the bonfire, not much business was done at this evening's meeting. Nonetheless I was able to chart the structure of these meetings, which are in three parts. First, a report is read detailing those who have been found guilty during the week of breaches to the rules and regulations, and listing how much, if anything, each is to pay in fines. The culprits are allowed to appeal. The next part of the meeting is reserved for those who have something to say and have put their names down on the list of speakers during the week. Finally, the best part is devoted to general discussion.

The meeting was got through swiftly and to the accompaniment of general uproar. One of the younger children had been tricked out of some money by one of the big boys. The younger one sobbed while the defendant made a great speech in his own defence, but his arguments were not convincing and he was condemned to instant repayment of the "loan". After that the assembly passed a resolution that no one must borrow money from anyone younger than himself. This proposal received the most support from the older children. At this point one small chap by accident broke his rocket and set up a roar that deafened us all. One of the girls ticked him off for disturbing the meeting, which she should never have done, because the tearful one at once went for her. However, she was the stronger, which only added insult to injury, and the meeting was interrupted for several minutes. One of the staff parted the two combatants and bore the little chap out, kicking and protesting wildly.

It is generally supposed that Summerhill is a parking place for difficult children, or the children of difficult parents; in other words, that it is a school for problem children. It is difficult to deny this, but it is still more difficult to confirm it. The school has acquired this reputation because, when it was started, in order to survive financially it had to take many difficult children. Moreover, schools that are not ordinary State or private schools, always risk being regarded as places for those with behaviour difficulties. One must remember, however, that there are difficult children everywhere. Otherwise it would not have been necessary, in Danish primary schools, to set up special classes of various kinds for them. As Neill's ideas gradually won a little ground, parents with "normal" children began sending them to Summerhill. Of course there still are problem children at the school, and there will always be. But I believe I could count the number of difficult children there now on one hand, though that would be risky, as I do not know each individual child. Now, problems seem mainly confined to the younger children, but of course it must be remembered that older children are better at concealment. One of the younger boys is a real exhibitionist and very aggressive. Apparently he prefers to pee when he can do so in public. At the end of today's meeting, he peed on the steps. The fact that he chose to do so where visitors could see him is illuminating. Ordinarily no one pays any great attention to his behaviour, but understandably the odd visitor might raise his eyebrows. However, at Summerhill the boy will have a fine chance of growing out of his problems. No one, of course, punishes him here for behaving like this; elsewhere, subjected to discipline in a milieu where there was compulsion, his "cure" would leave his problem unresolved.

Neill has not been well all day. Influenza. And yesterday Paul was in bed. Neill, however, was not too ill to see visitors. His daughter, Zoe, came to invite us across to his private quarters. He was sitting by the fire smoking like the damp firewood in it. "How did the meeting go?" he asked me, as I came in. "Pretty meagre," I said, "the children's heads were full of bonfire and fireworks." This obviously irritated Neill. The parliament was the school's image and it was by this that visitors to Summerhill judged it.

When we were all seated, Neill said: "My wife says I oughtn't to smoke so much, but I don't think I would be better if I gave it up. I am sorry I wasn't at this evening's meeting. It is the second time I have had to miss one because of illness, but I am not so ill that I can't answer questions. Have you any?"

"Does your staff usually stay with you? At the moment, I believe, there is only one who has been here any length of time."

"Unfortunately, they don't stay long. It is a pity for the children. They are often sorry when someone leaves. However, it is difficult to get staff to stay on. For one thing the salary is too small. I can only pay £20 a month, naturally including board, lodging and laundry, but that is too little for all the work involved. They all get the same salary, whether they teach or attend to the children in other ways. And age isn't taken into account either. My wife gets no more than the 19-year-old house-mother who looks after the tinies in the San. In the school's whole existence I have only once had to dismiss a master. But lots, of course, have left when they discovered they could not live up to the liberty this place guaranteed. A number have had something of their own to work off when they came here. I remember one who stopped washing and let his hair and beard grow, but he soon became tired of that. I don't interfere in the way the staff teach; they can do as they like and I have never eavesdropped outside a form-room door to hear what is going on inside. I wonder how many heads can say the same?"

"You gave us figures of salaries. How much does it cost to have a child at Summerhill?"

"That depends on the child's age, the financial situation of the parents, and whether there is more than the one in the family here. The fees vary between £300 and £500 a year. (1966) That is not particularly cheap, but even so it is cheaper for American parents to have their children at Summerhill, sending them to and fro across the Atlantic three times a year, than it is to send them to a private school in America. But for British parents it is expensive and it is only the well-off who can afford to spend so much on their children. That is something I can only regret. There is nothing to be done about it. The fact that Summerhill is so expensive is due to the fact that some children only pay half fees, and one or two can be here for nothing when there are special circumstances. Otherwise, all I can say is that the younger the child, the lower the fees."

"This school pays homage to the principle of freedom, but how is that to be understood? Is there nothing to which one has to say no?"

"I am so often faced with parents who want to give their children freedom—BUT! ... I shall leave out that little speciality, and concentrate on your good but difficult question. The public's idea of free children is that they spend their days smashing windows. That has nothing to do with it, of course. At Summerhill freedom means living your life without inconveniencing others or being inconvenienced by them. If children are first offered freedom when they are twelve or thirteen, they do not know what it means, and it will take them quite a while to discover that it does not mean doing exactly as one likes. You can convince yourself of that if you will just take a look at the noticeboard, where some of our laws are posted up, or by attending a Saturday meeting. As in every other system, we have law-breakers, but it is no exaggeration to say that the children here keep the law better than society does. That covers our domestic affairs, but of course there is a world outside Summerhill.

"A couple of years ago I spoke at a Saturday meeting about smoking. I have introduced a law forbidding children under sixteen to smoke. It is not easy to keep such a law or to see that it is carried out; nor does the fact that I and several members of the staff smoke make it any easier; but I had to introduce it because the Ministry had directed that all schools must ban smoking by minors because of the danger of lung cancer. Summerhill cannot be the only school in England not to do so. However, some who are under sixteen smoke and do so quite blatantly. Then I have to tell them: 'You can choose, you can either stay at the school and obey this rule, or leave it—and smoke as much as you like. I am compelled to observe the law. I won't punish you for smoking. The only thing I can do is to present you with this choice. You can call it a punishment if you like, but it is necessary for the law to be observed, for both my and your security. Don't think you can come here and do whatever you want. You can't.'

"Another thing: if here in England you could see on TV the American so-called horror comic films, I think I would forbid the children to see them. I would not allow such things here. I don't think it is fit for young chilren to be faced with all the perversities and morbidities that pass for entertainment. Anything like that is out with me, in the same way as I would not allow a Gestapo man on my staff. There are certain things one has to reject, and to protect oneself and others from.

"Some of you may have noticed that it says on the notice-board that visitors are not allowed to bring spirits for the children. Not so long ago I would have considered such a rule quite superfluous, as I imagine you all would. But unfortunately it did happen that one visitor, who had utterly misunderstood what we mean by freedom, brought some gin for the children. Hence the rule. And that has to appear on the board under the heading 'Guide-lines for Visitors'. Yes, of course, there are certain things to which one has to say no."

No one else had any questions and so most of us trooped off to the hockey pitch, where the bonfire was fighting a losing battle with the pouring rain. It did not even improve when Oliver poured a gallon of paraffin on what had been intended as a splendid blaze. The children were rather disappointed, but tried to console themselves with the fireworks, which fortunately went off beautifully. As bedtime came for the various age-groups the pitch became depopulated, and when pub time for the staff came round, the bonfire and the two armchairs were abandoned. It must be admitted that now the chairs really had had it!

We endured it in the pub until closing time at eleven o'clock. Our main topic of conversation was the departed American. Oliver said: "He was almost too keen. He came along as I was mending the roof over the lab. and my room, and asked if he could help. Pretty pushing for someone who had been at the school for only one hour. It was almost provocation. I declined the offer, in a friendly way, because I did not want to risk finding he had no idea how to mend a roof and so having to show him what to do. That would only have been a hindrance. But I do believe he took umbrage."

Peter had problems with his pupils: he was finding it difficult to get them to make the things portrayed in his album. Jane was wondering what to do about the next essay she set: should she let each of her pupils read out his essay and then have it criticized, or should she just comment on the theme and on the ways it had been treated?—one or two of the children had been rather hurt after the previous occasion's criticism. Paul was in philosophical mood, the philosophy being existentialist: how was it possible to be a free person under the damned yoke of this world? Harry's back was hurting and he must have been feeling like the Danish cartoonist's tramp who had a fly in his eye and was quite indifferent to the world situation. Two of the women were deeply in love; they were happy. And problems can be dispelled amazingly easily over a few drinks. (One day perhaps the Danish authorities will realize that problems grow in proportion to the tax on spirits.) Here, in the pub, we let off a little steam, stood our rounds and talked brilliantly. Just before closing time Oliver said: "Now we've drunk a quid's worth. That's pretty expensive." "Don't you believe it," I said. "In Denmark it would have cost us three quid." We suddenly felt immensely rich and got the barman to fill some stoppered bottles with strong brown ale, and this we drank in Oliver's den. Our tongues wagged and a gramophone churned out Bach into the small hours. In the end neither Jane nor Peter had any problems, but Paul was still in trouble with his existentialism.

Friday, November 11

Children swear and most grown-ups swear. Even so, some grown-ups wonder where children learn it all; perhaps they are not so much wondering as being tactful. Some people do not swear for reasons of religion, or because they think it bad manners, or not "nice". That would be all right if only they did not try to stop others swearing. Parents grumble when their offspring swear, and so do those who teach in our schools. When I was a boy, I was always being told that I must not swear. And when I defended myself by saying that my father swore, I was told that that did not matter as he was a grown-up. I could not see the logic of this, and have not been able to do so since. I cannot see what justification I would have for forbidding a child to swear, whether it was my own or someone else's. The farthest I can go is to ask a child to avoid using "ugly" words when someone who does not like them is present. There is no prohibition here, merely a somewhat philistine consideration for others that borders on hypocrisy, because such an attitude promotes the acceptance that there are taboo words. However, most grown-ups overlook the fact that swear words can be used in the service of pedagogy. To the child trained only to swear when grown-ups are out of earshot, it is a relief to find an adult, a master for example, who swears and so legalizes the use of swear words. This point of view fortunately is gaining ground, but it will probably be years yet before any one word is as good—or bad—as another.

Naturally the children at Summerhill swear, and no one tries to stop them. One thing appears to be characteristic: the children who have been there longest swear in the right places. Lars swears a great deal, almost everything he says being garnished with such a trump. Often he says "excuse me", and this makes me wonder, because I react neither to his swearing nor to his apologies. When, for a couple of days running, he had apologized for his bad behaviour, in order that I should realize he was not quite as bad as all that, I told him that if he could not swear without apologizing afterwards, it was almost too much of a business to do it at all. I assured him that it was all the same to me whether he did or didn't, and that it was so to the others at the school. Now he swears less—or perhaps I am not so quick to notice it.

Lars, being eleven, is awfully afraid of appearing childish and silly. He has several times said: "You think I'm silly, don't you?" He considers he is being childish when he swings from the rope in the big tree or when he chatters away about all and sundry. I have told him that if he had been twenty, I would have thought him silly, but he was scarcely that age yet. The other day, when we were walking round the grounds, he suddenly stopped and produced a matchbox from his pocket. I was to be shown his magnet and metal ladybird that would walk about a leaf when the magnet was moved round underneath the leaf. And then it came again: "You think I'm childish and silly, don't you?" I did not reply, but borrowed his toy and played with it. After a bit I handed it back, remarking that it was fun. "Isn't it," Lars said, "but it's still a bit childish to play with a thing like that when you're eleven".

Lars, of course, is one of the problem children here. Language difficulties prevent him having private lessons with Neill and also stop him playing with the other children. And just because he cannot, he doesn't even bother to think of doing so. To him the others are strange beings with whom he can only find fault. According to him the others in his room are quite impossible. They are after him, he says. It is evident that he would really like to invite me up, but dare not because of the others.

A few days ago he opened the door into his mad world. It is mad, because it is not a child's world. We were sitting on the floor in the little sitting-room, and he cross-examined me about life and death, heaven, hell and eternity, atom bombs, radiation, atomic-plants, fall-out, radioactive isotopes and degeneration as a result of radiation. And he ended his string of questions, and our conversation, with witches, the Brocken and frogmen. By the finish I was quite dumb and feeling thoroughly uncomfortable. There did not seem to be anything wrong with the boy's gifts and intelligence, rather the reverse. But the subjects occupying his mind were so abstract that very naturally he could not deal with them. To be frank I had a job answering too. He put his questions in a peculiar terminology, which I first had to interpret so that I could understand what he meant. He was confronted with thoughts greater than his vocabulary could cope with. And as the problems inherent in his questions were so complicated that they called for lengthy abstract explanations it is understandable that we were mostly talking at cross purposes. He could not understand many of the fumbling answers I gave. After an hour of this, I had to stop his barrage of questions by saying that my head was reeling and so, I imagined, his must be. I keep wondering who has forced him into this adult world of abstractions, mistrust of others, fear of displaying emotion in play, and terror of appearing "childish" and "silly".

By the afternoon he had replenished his armoury of questions: he began with sex. Sex, as he saw it, was dreadful filth, fascinating and repulsive; and he was much preoccupied with the strangeness of birth. He used the word "sex", but meant sexuality. "Look at that chap over there," he said, pointing to a boy of thirteen or fourteen, who was sitting talking to a girl. "He's very sexy—he goes round pawing the girls." I told him that I did not see anything wrong in that, if the girls did not mind. Lars did not think they did, because they were "sexy too". "Your room's upstairs," I said, "and I believe boys and girls are put together if they want. You use the same bathroom, too. Do you have girls in your room?" No, he certainly didn't. But when I asked whether in his heart of hearts he would not like to share a room with girls, he had to admit that he very much would, only I must not tell anyone. Naturally I promised that I would not.

After ridiculing the school's "oversexed" pupils for a bit, he suddenly changed the subject and touched on parts of Einstein's theory of relativity. He said: "If one moves with three times the speed of light, one becomes quite tiny and gets into one's mother's tummy." I dared not contest this, because I have never seen anyone in such a hurry, even though those under stress perhaps would like to be able to return to the foetus state. As he seemed intent on embarking on this bizarre notion, I decided a more practical approach was necessary. "Have you any sexy books in the school?" I asked. Yes, they had. I told him to go and fetch the sexiest. He went off to the library and returned with a book of sexual instruction called *He and She*. It was a book that could not possibly have fallen foul of the law, but it was to him "very sexy". He pumped me on the subject of male and female sexual organs and made a lot of nonsensical comments. Naturally, he tried to make it appear that he knew a lot and was not without some experience. I did not disillusion him altogether, because I believe that it is healthy for everyone to have a good idea of one's self. The world, I am sure, is not going to collapse spiritually earlier than physically, but if it should, that could be almost as dreadful. I remember a saying of Pascal's: "It is dangerous to let people see too clearly how like the animals we are without at the same time showing them our greatness." It is also dangerous to let man see his greatness too distinctly without seeing his baseness at the same time. But it is even more dangerous to let him remain ignorant of both. It is beneficial to show both sides. What I am afraid of is that one day people are going to realize that in certain spheres they rank lower than the animals. This is a fear that Pascal was spared, he did not experience the destructive tendencies of this century.

But I had to protest when Lars equated the womb with the bladder. Starting from here, I was able to tell him certain things about which he perhaps sought information without having asked. He did ask lots of questions concerning the illustrations in the book and I answered them; but before long he tired of listening. Then he returned the book.

There was to be a fancy-dress party that evening. I had promised Lars that I would come, and also that I would bring something for him. What I took was a piece of string in a matchbox. The two ends of the string were tied together. What could he do with this, he said. I began to show him how he could "cut his throat". He said: "Don't show me what to do. Just do it several times quickly and I'll see if I can discover the trick." I did the trick several times and then gave him the string. It wasn't long before he had discovered the secret.

The hall was full of bustle and noise. The children danced, shouted, leaped, chased each other and fought for fun. Lars did not take part in any of this, but went round "cutting throats". Some of the boys and girls of his own age wanted him to teach them the trick, but he was reluctant to divulge it. When he did, I noticed that he did say a few words of English. When he didn't know the words, he would pantomime. But by this time he could swear a bit in English.

On Thursday he began by questioning me about madness and mental deficiency, which he lumped together in a muddled way. I tried to sort out the muddle, but gave up when I discovered that he wanted to retain his prejudices. He went further and spoke of zoological curiosities, of people who were animals. I tried to apply the brake. He regards me as a rather stupid schoolmaster because I do not know the answers to all his questions. Suddenly he switched back to yesterday's subject, sex. Today he ventured further and questioned me about my sexual life. It seemed from his questions that he had left the smutty stage behind him, and as his questions seemed to be meant seriously, I answered those which I thought could be of help to him. Slowly his questions moved from "sexiness" to love. When he must have sensed that I would not think worse of him, he told me that he masturbated, adding very matter-of-factly, "You don't sperm until you're twelve or thirteen." But it was obvious that he was afraid of what might happen from doing this, so I tried to scotch all that nonsense, and he nodded and agreed, as if he had had the same idea the whole time. Then he embarked on the topic of "dirty books" and verbal graffiti. He had fallen for tales of super-sexual prowess, of which he spoke wide-eyed and in tones of awe. Wasn't it fantastic? Yes, indeed it was, and not a word of truth in it, either, I said. It is not often that fantasy outdoes reality; usually it is the other way round. I asked Lars if he couldn't get his father to send him some pornographic books—tolerable ones, I meant—but here he drew the line: he would never ask his father for that. Shortly afterwards he said: "At home we talk freely about everything—like here." He was evidently trying to patch over some of the holes in his own home conditions. One has met that before. I asked him how he knew that you could discuss anything at Summerhill. His parents in Oslo had told him that, and so had the inspector at the school he had attended there.

We went into the hall, where some of the small fry were playing. Lars dismissed them as "silly kids". One of the boys spoke to me and Lars at once asked: "What did he say?" He was naturally afraid of having his uncomplimentary remarks returned. I translated the boy's question, and as it did not concern Lars, he smiled condescendingly. Shortly afterwards a little girl, with a jerk of her head in Lars' direction, said: "He's my problem". I thought this magnificent and began to laugh. Lars immediately asked: "What did she say?" I translated and Lars smiled rather wanly. I added: "I think it is very nice of her to speak of you with such interest. It could mean that she feels friendly towards you." Lars tossed his head and strode off in dudgeon. The children watched him go, smiled and went on playing. They had not understood what Lars and I had said to each other, but they must have been aware of something.

Lars came back almost at once, as if nothing had happened. He said he would like to invite me into the library to show me some books. I realized that he wanted a private talk and suggested that he should invite me. But he just did not dare. "You mustn't go there," he said. "Oh, but I can, if I am invited." "I mustn't invite you." "Now, listen," I said, "the rules are the same for the library as for the dormitories —one is allowed in, if one is invited." "Yes, but I cannot invite you. I would be reported and they would talk about me at a meeting and I would have to pay money." We seemed to have reached an impasse. Then Olly, one of the house-mothers, passed us, a bundle of washing under her arm. I suggested to Lars that we ask her if he was allowed to invite me into the library or not. He agreed. I explained the situation to Olly, translating my questions and her answers, hoping that Lars would trust me here. Of course he was allowed to invite me, we were told, and Lars declared himself satisfied.

We were the only ones in the library. I was right, there wasn't any book Lars wanted to show me. He settled himself on the sofa and off he went: "Perhaps you won't believe it, but the world is such an extraordinary place, there are people who can walk without your hearing them. They glide across the floor. And some can talk with people on other planets." I was all ears. This sounded exciting. And Lars explained, awkwardly, stuttering, but as enthusiastically as if he was a prophet. He spoke of becoming "clear". When you were "clear" you could do many supernatural things. His mother used to go for exercises, because you have to practise a lot to become clear, and sometimes she had taken Lars with her so that he should become clear. As far as I could understand, Lars' father had refused to have anything to do with such nonsense. Was I right in seeing here a hint of the crazy creature, whose traces I had come across now and then: one of those people with hypertension, for whom mysticism has become a religion, a more modern way of escape than the old-fashioned form of praying to God and going in awe of His wrath in the hope of getting to Paradise; a religion of nuclear satellites, for those who hope to be rescued at the eleventh hour from the mushroom clouds by a spaceship from a remote planet; a religion for those who practise meditating themselves into a state of indifference—and disintegration. No one would object to Lars' mother gliding about the floors in her home, being so relaxed she never lost her temper with her son or was cold to her husband, or even having pen-friends on Mercury or Pluto—as long as she didn't take the boy into her crazy world to let him have a chance of becoming "clear". But there is no law that forbids parents to destroy their children intellectually—and, what is worse, no such law could be formulated. Parents are here left to their common sense, which is frequently a very poor guide.

What can one do with such a boy? Could Summerhill help to put things right?

Lars had got quite worked up, and I had no idea how to cope with the situation. I tried to make him slow down—to act as a retro-rocket and parachute, so that his capsule should not burn out on its return to earth. Gradually I succeeded. "That was exciting," I said at the end of our space-flight and talk together.

Lars wanted to see my room at the hotel and fished politely for an invitation. It was not often he was in the little town. His mother could not come from Oslo to see him every weekend. I suggested that tomorrow we go for a walk in the town and end up at the hotel for a talk in my room. But having got his invitation, Lars began to have misgivings. He did not think he was allowed outside the grounds. So I took him over to the noticeboard and translated the relevant notice; that helped. "But," he said, "I mustn't go outside the grounds before 12 o'clock." He was right. The English police keep a sharp look out for children alone on the streets before twelve o'clock in case they are playing truant from the schooling that is considered so very necessary for them and thus risking not making anything of their lives! But he was not going to be alone, I was intending to be with him, and it was unlikely that we would go for our walk before twelve o'clock. "So you'll come and fetch me tomorrow," he said with his mouth full of banana, hand raised in a gestured goodbye. We had just been to the tuck shop for supplies; the tuck shop is strategically placed at the very entrance to Summerhill. The children are free to pay it a visit at any time of the day and can do so without going outside the grounds. It has a huge turnover.

I told Harry that Lars would be out for two or three hours and off we went. When we reached the main street, Lars became more and more agitated. He kept as far from the edge of the pavement as he could, and whenever I paused to look in a shop window, he glanced round him on all sides. On the second occasion that he took cover in the doorway of a shop for no apparent reason, I asked him what was wrong. He told me he thought he had seen two of the Summerhill pupils. I asked him to explain. Apparently he was afraid of meeting any of the others in case they reported him for being outside the grounds; then his name would come up at a meeting. I gave up the idea of explaining that our jaunt was entirely legitimate. He had understood that with his mind, but emotionally he hadn't. Although he had had it all explained, he was still panic-stricken. So I took him quickly to the hotel and up to my room.

No sooner was Lars inside the room than he began opening drawers. He did not ask if he might, but just set about doing so systematically. I did not stop him; I had no reason to give for telling him not to. As soon as he had seen what each drawer contained, he shut it and went on quickly to the next. I did not speak, but just sat watching him. He did not say anything either. Then he drank some of my soda water, again without asking if he might, and ate a banana. All this took place in profound silence. He was certainly an easy guest. I sat there eager to see what he would do next.

A bundle of sheets of paper with handwriting on them lay on the chest of drawers. He began rummaging among the papers, and once or twice his gaze paused on a certain area of the paper. It was not very likely that he would be able to read my writing, and if he did manage to read something, he would not be able to understand it. But he would probably begin to be sarcastic about it, so as to try to give me the impression that he had understood—to make me sit open-mouthed and admire his fantastic capabilities. And he would talk a lot of drivel, as he had done yesterday, and that would be tiring for us both. So I took the papers from him and placed them in a drawer, saying that they were for me only and that what I had written did not concern others, at any rate until I perhaps chose to let it. He was not in the least put out, but asked cheerfully if I had ever written for children. I had to disappoint him, admitting that I didn't have any boys' books about horse-thieves, detectives or smugglers. But for younger children, I told him I had a small arsenal of tall stories of my own invention in my head. He asked me to tell one, and I did so, a simple little tale which has had success with four-year-olds. That he said it was good, does not matter; what does is the fact that he was engrossed by it. I was really rather surprised because it was absolutely free of any of the ingredients which seemed so to preoccupy him as to make life difficult for him. But perhaps that was why.

So far he had done most of the questioning; I thought it might be fun to exchange roles for a while. I asked him what classes he went to. I had asked him this before, and I was interested to hear if he would answer differently now. I had never seen him in class: no matter what time of day I went up to the school, he was there and had time for a chat. Well, he said, he went to English, handwork and science. He went to science because sometimes things went BANG there. So his original long list of classes had now been reduced to three. What did he do in English classes, I asked. Oh, he wrote essays and dictation. That was an obvious whopper, but I did not say anything. There's no reason to keep telling people they are liars; they know it perfectly well. I said that I was surprised he stayed at Summerhill when he was bored there, disliked most of the other children and did not like the place as a whole, these all being things he had previously told me in so many words. Summerhill was a free school, I said, and I was surprised he did not see that he was given the money for a single ticket back home. He was free, wasn't he, to leave the school; I had the impression that he had not been sent there. That was true, he had himself elected to go to Summerhill, and he wanted to stay. So then I more or less ticked him off for going to lessons. He would do much better just to play with the other children; that was the way to learn English, and he would not like Summerhill until he had. He stared at me as at a presumptuous idiot, and told me that he went to school to learn something. What did I think he would become, if he could not read by the time he was fourteen? I had to be careful about retaliating here. I have known children who could read when they were five and they haven't turned out anything very much, and I know one person who was fourteen before he could read and now is twenty-two and studying for a degree. But to have told Lars that would just have confused him, so I shrugged and left it at that. And yet, what does one understand by "being able to read"? Read what? A strip cartoon, or Kierkegaard? And what does one mean by "becoming something"? Each can strike his own balance here. People are notoriously happy in their faith; but to that one could add that not all who are happy have faith.

I had realized for a long time that I did not enjoys Lars' full confidence, and I was not going to court it or hope for it. If he gave it me, well and good; if not, I would only have myself to blame. What I had not fully realized, however, though I had sensed it, was that he identified me to some extent with the authority he must have encountered in his short life. It was obvious: I was one of the many grown-ups who thought that you could only become something if you went to school and learned to read, etc. To save the situation, and get a stage further, I decided to play my cards dashingly. Do or die! So I told him why he was so dissatisfied and fed up—it was because he thought and talked about things which were far beyond his ability to comprehend. And I recited at random a few subjects that were beyond even me. Then something happened. Lars became really angry. And I was glad, because a good friendship often starts with a thorough-going row. Why was I meddling in his affairs? he wanted to know. I had no right to do so. Very well, I said, but neither have you any right to meddle in mine. Yesterday you asked me a lot of personal questions and today you looked at my papers to see what I had been writing. I suppose you want to know about me, which is fine, for I want to get to know you. He admitted I was right: he had meddled. I then told him that I had nothing against his doing so, but that he must be prepared for me to say "no" at times, as I already had, and naturally he had the same right to stop me, as he had just done. And I went on: "If you don't like the conversation, let's stop it now. We'll be just as good friends if we do." "I can't bear the way you talk," he said, looking all injured innocence. I smiled at him and said that I had embarked on this because I was getting a bit tired of seeing him depressed and bored. He did not reply to that. I suppose I ought to have been more clever and said something psychologically more appropriate, but this is what I did say. This produced a pause in hostilities. To gain more time, I filled my pipe, making a great business of it. I felt as if we were stuck.

It was Lars who broke the silence, telling me that I ought to write about what was "good". I could have put us both in a painful situation by asking how he knew that that was not what I did, but luckily I did not fall into that trap. Instead, I asked him what he thought was "good". "Well," he said, "something about a little girl who goes into the woods to pick flowers and looks at the sun and watches the sunset —and that sort of thing." "All right, but what is 'bad'?" I asked. "Bad is violence, crime and detective stories." "I see." Didn't I agree with him? I didn't, and I told him so. I said, too, that I could not explain off-hand what was bad and what good. He was bound to misunderstand a lot and get confused over all sorts of things. Lars felt rather hurt that I was refusing to talk "philosophy" with him. He was so accustomed to that at home, and I saw no reason to make things worse by doing so. Anyway, why should I accept his definition of evil and good? If I had said he was right, I would only have confirmed him in the belief that he himself was evil. When we were together, he had entertained me with little else but violence, crime and detective stories. Nicely served, of course, but the tendency was clearly there: indirectly he was wallowing in his own definition of wickedness, because earlier he had, one supposed, had his nose rubbed in it.

We sat silent for a while, then he said something which made me realize that on the first day we met I had made a capital blunder. I was wrong in having asked him what he thought of the place. And here, of course, he was clearly right. In my thoughtlessness I had started his relationship to me on a lie. At the time he had more or less said that he liked being at Summerhill. What other reply could he have given? He did not know me. What I had done was exactly the same as when one asks someone, "How are things?" and he replies, "Fine." And things can just as well be awful. We all know the situation, and among adults it does no harm because they know that these are empty phrases; but to a child such words have value. It is not so much the words themselves that count, as the feeling, the attitude behind them. By asking that, I had unwittingly set myself up as authority—and with authority you have to bluff. I admitted to him unreservedly that I had behaved idiotically. There was nothing to say. Explanation would not mean anything to him. They would only be excuses that I was using to cover up. It was at this point I realized that Harry was absolutely right: it was I should have said what I thought about the school. I was not in his shoes. If the school seemed good to me, to him, knowing my attitude, it would naturally only be worse, because I was a grown-up —and authority.

When we were walking back to the school, he questioned me about my schooldays and wanted to know what sort of a person my father was. He was poking his nose in with a vengeance and I was glad that he was. He had not given me up altogether. We had a chat about good and bad schoolmasters. He was very interested in hearing about the strict masters I had had to do with—or they with me, depending on where the emphasis was laid—and I gladly told him about the specimens of the breed in whose clutches I had been. This provided an opportunity to tell him by way of contrast something of the good ones I had known and knew. What I gave, of course, was a picture of a Summerhill master, but having learned by experience, I left the word "Summerhill" out of it. He listened without interrupting. Then we talked about beating. Walking up the drive, he told me that his father used to beat him when he was small.

On Thursday, when I was having a cup of tea in the common room during morning break, I asked Jane, who teaches English to Lars' class, if Lars did go to her lessons. She laughed. "Has he been trying to tell you that one? Don't you believe it! He's never put a foot inside the class-room for any of my lessons." Paul said that he occasionally came to a science lesson, if he knew there were going to be experiments. These were the most exciting, and that was perfectly all right. Peter said that now and again Lars would look in at the workshop and play with a piece of wood, but never did anything with it. Neill did not say anything; he just sat smiling wryly and looking at a catalogue from a firm of publishers in Oslo. Harry added that Lars sometimes came into the art room and ruined a piece of paper. I could tell from the tone of their voices that the staff were slightly indignant about the way Lars never went to classes. That was understandable. Those who teach at Summerhill have mostly come from schools where attendance is compulsory. It calls for a radical change of attitude on whether they go to classes or not, if you are to achieve anything with Summerhill pupils. The Summerhill staff has to accept completely the voluntary principle and the fact that they must not interfere in the child's personal choice, nor try to influence it to abandon a point of view which is the child's and the child's alone. This calls for a certain period of adjustment, and as most of the staff do not stay particularly long, you get the impression that several have yet to adjust to this special kind of school.

I have tried to compare the Summerhill staff with the majority of Danish schoolmasters and mistresses I know. The comparison is very much in the former's favour. Most Danish schoolmasters and mistresses suffer from a morbid passion for work. They wail if they have a period taken from them, even, quite often, in the so-called progressive schools. If, for practical reasons, their Christmas holidays have to be made one day longer than in the primary schools, you will find them working on an Easter or Whitsun public holiday. Many seem to think that the world is coming to an end if they can't have their classes on the King's birthday: no one pays any attention to the Queen's birthday—I suppose she will have to campaign like other women for so-called equality of rights. If a schoolmaster falls ill, there is the dreadful problem of who can take his classes, because "the children can't sit there on their own, can they?" They cannot, but is that their fault? The staff all drive themselves through the school year because time is short, and the curriculum large, and the children idle, while the Ministry expects ... In Danish schools the staff drives itself to crabbedness and misanthropy. Now, this last week, there had been a lot of 'flu about, and at Summerhill a couple of the staff had caught it. They went to bed, leaving their classes to look after themselves. There was no racking of brains as to who should replace them. When a master is ill, the children have the time off. It is all very logical.

I told Harry that Lars and I would probably pay him a visit during the day. He smiled and nodded.

We talked about Lars and how he should feel reasonably at home if only he could speak English, and I suggested that from this day on I would try to speak only English with him. To all intents and purposes there was no language difficulty where the two of us were concerned. Occasionally

I might have to explain something, but on the whole Lars understood Danish perfectly well. To me there was no doubt that languages came easily to him. The boy was really quite gifted and so I thought that my suggestion would work. The others thought it a good idea and only regretted that I had not had it earlier, for I did not have much longer there.

Just before the bell went, Neill shoved the Norwegian publisher's catalogue across to me and asked what was said there about his book, *Summerhill School*, which had been published in a cheap edition. Nothing but praise, I told him, and I could see that this pleased him. A bit of a sop after the American's letter and the rather disordered Saturday meetings.

When I came out of the common room Lars was standing in the hall watching a game that was going on. I said a few sentences in English. He stared at me. I said one or two more. Then he laughed. Encouraged by this, I said quite a lot in English. He answered with the ten or fifteen words of English that he knew. On I went, but it quickly became too much for him, and he threatened to go away unless I talked in a tongue he could understand. If he walked off as a protest, the game would be up, as it would be if I could only carry out my intention to a minor extent. I told him therefore that if it made him want to go, it was better I didn't talk so much to him in English, but on the other hand I was not going to promise not to talk English to him again.

I asked him why he wasn't in class. He wasn't feeling like it today, he said. It could be interesting to see what excuses he would make during the next few days, though it was, of course, possible that he was animated by a general dislike of classes. Then, in Danish, I gave him a curtain-lecture on the necessity of attending classes and learning things, so that he could become something, etc., etc. I made it as silly as possible because I wanted to make him laugh: to roar with laughter. I had never heard him laugh really: he would only go "ha-ha" and contort himself as if he had cramp. But now he laughed properly. "Oh, oh—you're being your father. That's what your father must have said to you." And he hastened to add: "But you don't really mean it, do you?" I was able to reassure him. I went on playing the fool and he laughed again. When I couldn't think of anything more to say, we went to the art room, I having suggested we should do a painting together. He laughed a lot at that. He discarded several subjects before deciding on the Hermitage palace and park, which had made a great impression on him once when he was in Denmark. He painted the building, a stag and the grass, while I did the trees, the sun and the sky. It was great fun and Lars laughed a lot. He protested strongly when I painted two rings, one green and one blue, on his grass. This was not because I was trespassing, but because I had already painted one sun and there weren't three suns, nor did you get suns on the grass. These are objections you usually encounter only from opponents of art subsidies, people who want only what they see to be reproduced—and nothing besides. So I did not take his criticisms seriously, but I told him that these circles were wheels. I had put the park on wheels. Had he never seen it on wheels? This was a kind of humour he could understand. I was being just as silly as he, and it is always nice to have a fellow sufferer.

Eventually, when we had finished our joint effort, Lars wanted to paint a picture on his own. I was not to interfere. He wanted to paint something abstract. And what else could he have wanted to do? His entire world was abstract, and everyone, I imagine, creates out of his own conception of life. First he painted the paper all over with a ground colour of turbid grey-blue-green. Then he soaked some brushes in different colours and sloshed these over the paper in streaks and blotches. Jackson Pollock has done this better. There was nothing childish in what Lars did; but it was just an imitation of an adult world. Perhaps we ought to paint more pictures together.

When I said good-bye, he asked the inevitable: "Are you coming again tomorrow?"

Saturday, November 12

It is not always easy for the Saturday meeting's chairman to enforce the respect for free speech required in a democracy. The small fry often disturb the proceedings and sometimes the damper has to be put on the spirits of even the older ones. Going to the meetings is quite voluntary; if you like you can leave in the middle, or come in the middle, as long as the coming and going does not obstruct freedom of speech and the meeting's institutions. Sometimes it is touch and go. As a rule the small fry are turned out when they make so much noise that one cannot hear oneself speak. It is very seldom they leave the meeting voluntarily. The older ones do, however. It seems to be rare for them to be turned out. They go when they feel insulted or provoked, or when they are bored.

Today's meeting was mainly concerned with the sale of clothing. It had transpired that in order to raise cash a couple of the younger ones had sold gloves, socks and scarves —even a woollen sweater. The fit did not seem to have mattered, for the purchasers had all been bigger children. At Summerhill there is financial inequality. As such it is perhaps scarcely worth mentioning, for the same thing exists in all societies. Everyone cannot have the same amount of money and never will have. It is also questionable whether it would be socially advantageous if they did. But that's not our concern. We can leave the capitalists and socialists to fight over that. At Summerhill, however, there seems to be an enormous gulf, and this is a source of irritation. The children from the United States are Croesuses compared with the English children. That, perhaps, is a reason for such lively dealings on "change". Such things as watches and bicycles do not seem to hold any particular value for the American children. Why, then, is there trading in relatively worthless textiles? This is just another aspect of the poverty-wealth business: at the end of the week the well-off children seldom have more than their poorer comrades and so they have to turn something into cash. There were several cases of clothes having been bought and sold this week, and each was discussed individually. Everyone concerned had his say and spoke without reluctance or nervousness. This is a problem that had cropped up before and there was a law that one was not allowed to sell one's clothes. This law had been passed out of consideration for parents, who have to know what clothes their children have. Also there is the human aspect, e.g. the scarf that Granny knitted. It was an excellent law, but one that was broken on occasion when finances were low. On this occasion there were a number of law-breakers and therefore the meeting was content to hand out serious warnings, emphasizing the law, and to see that everything was handed back.

A boy of Lars' age, perhaps a room-mate, wanted to speak, and told the meeting that Lars had had his yellow scarf stolen. At all events, he was unable to find it. Lars squinted up at me and smiled when his name was mentioned in a context that was not in any way compromising. It transpired that one of the smaller boys had "just borrowed it". The case did not take up much time and it was not thought necessary to fine the borrower. Lars was asked if he wanted to pursue the matter and require compensation, but he didn't. Here I acted as communications-link. This fact prompted Ena to raise the question whether it would not be a good thing to appoint one of Lars' contemporaries to act as a sort of house-father for him. Lars protested. Ena smiled and nodded persuasively, and I whispered soothing words into his ear. The argument in favour of the arrangement was that Lars still found difficulty in talking to the others and such a house-father could be his liaison with the various functions of the school until such time as Lars knew enough English to manage without him. Everyone thought this an excellent arrangement and one boy, who volunteered, was appointed Lars' house-father. This was not done with Lars' consent and I am not convinced that it was right to have done it. On the other hand, nor am I convinced that there was not a danger of Lars slipping more and more into isolation. So, all things considered, it was probably the most sensible thing to have the house-father.

At the subsequent meeting with Neill, he was asked why Latin figured in the time-table. It was surely not necessary to learn Latin so early, and anyway who was interested in Latin? "Does Latin figure in the time-table?" Neill looked bewildered. I nodded, and he went on: "I was not aware that there was Latin in the time-table. I don't draw it up. One of the staff does that, and I never meddle with teaching. I have my classes and I take them. Beyond that I am not particularly well up in what is done, either with the time-table or in classes. All I know is that it all goes very well. And that satisfies me. Nor do I know exactly which children go to which classes, but I do know who bullies others."

This caused a mirthful stir. Fancy a headmaster who did not know what subjects figured in his time-table. I, however, knew the reason for Latin being taught, as Oliver had told me only a few days before. Seeing it in the time-table had startled me and, as Oliver happened to be passing the notice-board at that moment, I asked him about it. It transpired that it was Oliver himself who had included it at the request of some of his biology pupils, who wanted to learn the different Latin terms along with the English. It was thus a question of technical Latin and not Caesar's wars, Cicero's orations or Hannibal's elephants. This I now communicated to the smiling meeting.

"There you are. Here's a visitor who's been here a month and he knows something I didn't know, though I have been here since 1921. Well—we didn't have Latin then either!"

The last remark aroused general mirth. Here at last was a headmaster who did not mistake himself for a time-table and did not suffer from split personality. I had the impression that the visitors liked the company of this old school rebel. And it was mutual.

"How long do children stay at Summerhill as a rule?"

There was no mirth in the questioner's voice and Neill's expression became serious too.

"There's no rule. Some come here at seven or eight and leave when they are sixteen. Some are here only a few years. The most irritating thing is when parents take their children away from Summerhill when they have been put right and are enjoying being here. The excuse for doing this is generally that they now want to send them to a school where they can learn something. I don't bother much about this as a vote of no confidence in the school, but I am sorry for the child, because as a rule it means the child is going to be unhappy when it is put back in the same surroundings which previously had resulted in its having to be sent to Summerhill. We have a case in point at the moment. This is a Canadian boy who came here eighteen months ago. He was nervous and unhappy. The school he had just left was one of the usual authoritarian kind, where on occasion you got thrashed. Further, his parents had brought him up very strictly. He got all right in about a year and is now profoundly unhappy at leaving us. What is one to do in such cases? My wife had a talk with him yesterday and he confided to her that he did not want to go back to Canada with his parents. 'But what shall I do?' he asked her, in tears. It is not pleasant to know that a child is unhappy and we cannot help him because we don't have the powers of guardians here. My wife told him that when his parents come to fetch him, he should kick and shout and say that he didn't want to go home. Naturally, that won't help, because his parents have made up their minds that the time has come for the boy to learn something. But if he does as my wife suggested, he will at least be reacting in the way natural to him in such a situation, and also his parents must then realize that he does not want to leave and that his protest means something."

"Don't parents often interfere in their children's schooling to the extent of questioning them about what they are learning—in a word, influencing the child to choose certain subjects or all the subjects a child of the same age would learn at ordinary schools?"

"The school makes it a condition for acceptance of a child that parents refrain from trying to influence their child to take certain subjects, either by talking or writing about it. Parents know all about this. If they do not follow these instructions, there is no point in sending their children here, because the child will still be under the authoritarian dictatorship of the home, which is what it has come to Summerhill to avoid. Fortunately it is very rare for parents to try to influence their children while they are here. In other words, they accept our order and arrangements. At the moment we have here a very gifted girl who, when she first came, was quite disinterested in lessons. However, she wasn't bored, a thing children seldom are anyway, when they have been here a short time. She occupied herself with various ploys. She did not bother anyone and was allowed to get on with things in peace and quiet. She was soon very pleased to be here: she was frank and obliging and everyone liked and enjoyed having her. Then all at once a change came over her. She became nervous and sullen and avoided us as far as possible. I wondered a lot what could have caused this change, and one day I discovered the reason: the girl confided in me, telling me about the pressure her father was putting on her. She showed me a few of his latest letters. In them he reproached her for not going to lessons, and as good as demanded a promise that she would start schoolwork so as not to drop too far behind. I wrote at once to the father, reminding him of the conditions on which we had accepted his child. I told him of the change in his daughter's behaviour and explained what had caused it. I ended my letter by requiring either that he stopped putting pressure on his daughter or that he take her back home. I had a very swift reply full of apologies and a promise that he would not require his daughter to do school-work. And he kept his promise. The girl recovered and almost a year to the day after coming here she began going to most lessons. Today she attends all the lessons in her class and is one of the brightest pupils we have."

Monday, November 14

I had scarcely entered the door today before a little girl accosted me. With eyes upturned, she began making up to me and said:

"Give me sixpence!"

"I'm not allowed to."

"Give me threepence!"

"I'm not allowed to."

"Give me a penny!"

"That's forbidden!"

"Give me a halfpenny!"

"That's forbidden ..." (she walked away) "... and you know it."

"Yes."

If it comes off, so much the better. Most of the children turn their pocket-money into sweets the moment they get it. What else should they buy?

My visit to the school today had a limited objective. I wanted to try to get the older ones' agreement for a group interview. What I was particularly interested in finding out was how they managed the liberty they presumably were able to enjoy in sexual matters. This was a sphere in which no regulations had been promulgated and there were no locked doors between the sexes—except such as they naturally locked themselves. The world regards sexuality as a problem, and I wanted to try to lead off with this and see where we would get. I hoped that the discussion would provide an explanation of why so far there had not been a case of pregnancy at the school. Perhaps Denmark's traditional boarding-school system could learn a little wisdom on the subject, instead of finding nothing else to do but expel pupils who had intercourse—or were on the way to doing so. That, naturally, does not solve any problems, but causes a lot more.

When I last met the older children in the converted railway coach, I had not told them what I intended to interview them about, only that I could envisage a short or long discussion depending on how we all felt. My reason for this was that I did not want them to come prepared. This might perhaps distort their answers. They might have taken me in. Also, I know that many people had asked them a lot of questions about this, and that they did not particularly like it.

I went across to the railway coaches to see if I could find out what date and time might suit. The boys were very obliging, but again referred me to the recurring discussions with Neill and Eva. Although I had been at Summerhill almost a month, I had not been at one of these, which were supposed to be a Thursday institution, as Harry had told me, which meant that I could attend them. Unfortunately, Ena was now in bed with influenza, so that probably there would not be much discussion. I had a feeling that the little ruffians were fighting shy of the idea. But why? They asked me how long I was to be there still. A whole month—oh, well, I really ought to be able to come to a discussion. But was there any guarantee there would be a Thursday discussion during the next four weeks? No, there wasn't. I then explained that I would love to come and talk with them at such a meeting, but there was no necessity for Ena and Neill to be there.

They could regard our talk as a "period", to which they could come or stay away as they liked. Yes and well and oh, perhaps. It wasn't so simple, you see. Why not? Well, they would rather have one of the grown-ups from the staff there to prevent disturbances. This bewildered me. Was this a free school or was it a disciplined run-of-the-mill place? I told them that if we held the meeting without anyone from the staff being at it, I would tell any possible disturbers of our peace to clear out: I was pretty good at this. But no—they preferred to have Neill there. He could perhaps help them, if they found it difficult to answer my questions.

And that was as far as I got. I went back to the hotel and pondered. I still pinned my hopes on two things: that Ena would soon be up and about again, and that there would be a discussion evening before I left.

Tuesday, November 15

Everyone knows the situation of being faced with an apparently insoluble task, which you cannot think of any way of accomplishing. Then suddenly, perhaps the next day, the solution appears of itself. All at once there it is: the solution comes as a gift after you have given up. That's what happened to me today.

I found Wood leaning against the shoring where they are excavating what one day will be a swimming-pool. The last few days had been frosty, and before that it had rained, so the work was halted for the rest of the year at least. I went up to Wood, hoping for a chat. Naturally we began by talking about the swimming-pool. When it was finally finished, there was to be a ten-foot fence round it with two doors that could be locked, and no one was to be allowed to use the pool unless a member of the staff was present. At night there would be a cover over the water. I was surprised that Wood could state this so categorically, for I gathered the matter had not yet been discussed in the parliament. Was this freedom or what?

He told me that Summerhill was not what it had been. That remark made me prick up my ears. With his hand Wood described a curve in the air. "This is Summerhill," he said. "Sometimes it is down in a trough, sometimes on the crest of a wave." At present the school was in a trough, and not what it had been five years previously. Wood ought to know, for he is Neill's stepson. He came to the school as a five-year-old and stayed there until he was seventeen. Then he trained in ceramics for a couple of years and had now come back. Wood explained Summerhill's curve. The reason for the present trough was that many of the pupils had been there too short a time to comprehend and live Summerhill life. Just two years before, there had been only twenty-one pupils. Then Neill's book had been a best-seller in the U.S.A., which had produced a surge of pupils from America. The members of the committees whose jobs it was to see that the motions accepted by parliament were carried out, were either too young or did not comprehend what a free school signified and the responsibility it laid upon them, because they had not yet been there long enough. It was a great loss for Summerhill when a group of pupils who had been there since they were five or seven, left at the age of fourteen or sixteen, as had happened two years before. In four or six years time Summerhill would be on another crest, because then the small fry in San and Carriage would be big enough to set the lead. And the big boys in the railway coaches (who wanted to have Neill and Ena at their side to pull their chestnuts out of the fire) would have long since dispersed into "life's treadmill", as Harry called life after Summerhill.

These factors also play a part when discussing sexual subjects. At present, most pupils are far from being free enough to be able to deal with these as they ought to be dealt with. It was thus very fortunate that I had not revealed to the older children what I was hoping we would discuss at our group interview. Ena and Neill talk to them on sexual subjects, but it is not easy to get close to them when they are blocked. Neill would also have liked to discuss these subjects with the staff so that they should know what his views here were, but unfortunately for the time being the composition of the staff was such that this was not possible. Here again it was a question of a number of them not having been at the school more than a year at the most. But, Wood added, there had been many periods when it was possible to discuss sex with the staff—even when they had not been there particularly long. Naturally it did not depend solely on that. The young pupils at Summerhill were free to play their sexual games unhindered and to vary them as imagination or desire prompted. When the time came for the games to be more "realistic", Neill simply had to compromise with his principles, otherwise the school would be closed. So he talked to the older ones, explaining that if a girl became pregnant there, the school would have to close down. The pupils respected this, and the school is still open. If this isn't calibre in a headmaster, then I don't know what calibre is. The argument is quite clear, simple and understandable: if the school was to be shut down, all those there would suffer—as would all the others who would have gone to it later.

Wednesday, November 16

It is likely that if the Danish authorities did not worry so much about the height of ceilings and whether there was main drainage, the housing problem would be reduced considerably. The English authorities apparently do not concern themselves with Summerhill. If they did, a couple of the staff would be homeless. As it is, there is no accommodation problem for the staff. All have a roof over their heads, though the roof may vary considerably in quality. You must not expect too much of accommodation at Summerhill; the school's finances do not allow much to be done. But you can live there and you can survive the winter. Neill's own accommodation is the best, and the newest. He has a whole house, a bit bigger than a Danish one-family house. But then he has a family, which none of the staff has, and he is not able to move. In the grounds, among the tall tufts of grass, is Olly's cross between a dormobile and a tool-shed. One day, when Lars and I were walking in the grounds, Lars went in a wide curve round Olly's little place. The explanation was that Olly did not like people near it. That was what Lars said and possibly he was right; but it was equally possible that for one reason or another Olly had been included among the things and people he feared. Olly lived next to his class-room where he mainly taught biology. Class-room and dwelling together comprised a little outhouse and made me think of the old Danish country schoolmaster, now presumably no more, who lived and did his splendid work in a house with only a couple of rooms, so that it was difficult to decide what was a class-room and what his home. Oliver's room was not large. After making three large built-in cupboards, there was just room for a bed, a small table, two chairs, a little bookcase and a radio gramophone. He certainly felt cramped there. The other evening in the pub he was saying that he might buy a house nearby, so presumably he was counting on staying some years at Summerhill. He likes it there, and the house move is more an escape from the pub, where you can so easily spend ten shillings an evening, than from the school.

The three house-mothers have their rooms in the sections which they have to look after: San, Carriage and the upstairs of the main building. They do not live there to control the children, but to attend to them when the need arises, as most mothers do. They see to the children's clothes, help bath them if necessary, play with them, see they get their food, and so on. The dining-room is not big enough for all sixty-two to eat in together, so the tinies eat on their own. Paul, Jane, Ulla, Peter and Wood have rooms somewhere or other in the school buildings, though they are not near the pupils to keep an eye on them. It may well be that they are disturbed at times by the noise the children make, but of course there is no law to say that they may not ask the children to pipe down if they get too noisy.

And then there's Harry's house. This is joined on to the theatre, so one can say that he really enjoys peace as long as the theatre is locked. It's many years since I saw *The Gold Rush*, but as far as I can remember Charlie Chaplin's house in the wilds was very like Harry's hut. Two years ago it was on the point of collapsing, but a visitor who could wield a hammer and nails saved the situation. Harry lives best of the staff, but then he will soon be celebrating his jubilee. As I've said, there is no difference in salary between members of the staff, but there is in accommodation. And that has to be. Pound notes are things you can count and it is merely a question of seeing that the same number goes into each envelope; but for everyone to have the same standard of accommodation, they would have to build identically for all, which would require an investment beyond the resources of Summerhill. So the staff is accommodated as and where there is room. And there would not be any objection if a member of the staff brought his own dwelling, of one kind or another, and set it up in the grounds.

Harry's hut is dirty, untidy and battered. Cobwebs festoon the pointed roof, and the doors hang awry. A stove gives off a good heat. On the walls are many pictures painted by either pupils or Harry himself, and round about are pieces of sculpture. Harry keeps diving into the other room to fetch interesting or amusing things which he has found, made or been given. One day he showed me five stones he had found on the beach. The intriguing thing about these stones was that by arranging them in a certain way they were like a recumbent woman. Not only that, but you could make one of the woman's legs either bend or stretch out straight, depending on the way you arranged one of the stones. Harry's hut is a place where you can be happy and rejoice. As you do, the mess disappears. But the cobwebs don't disappear; I believe Harry collects them.

Monday, November 21

Harry is the first among equals in his art room. His right to teach—if that's what you call it—does not come from having passed a pedagogic exam but from the possession of artistic maturity. He paints, models, sculpts, saws, files, and so forth, himself. This reminds me of the question Neill asked the other evening: "Why is it so few English teachers have written good books? After all, they teach the language." In Denmark the same applies to teachers of Danish, and perhaps even more to our creative artists. Why are there so few creative artists teaching in Danish schools? The answer is simply trade union dictatorship. The teachers' union in Denmark does not look kindly upon anyone who has not been to a training college. For a painter or a sculptor to get a teaching job, he has to have this essential certificate. Another of Neill's sayings is: "If Picasso came to Leiston wanting to teach art at the Grammar School, they would not take him on." Indeed, the world is a silly place: those who can are seldom allowed to do.

Harry was fortunate in that he had found his niche in life at Summerhill, well away from pettiness and intolerance. His work is quite demanding because when the children are energetic and interested it is not only small things they tackle. Before the Christmas and summer holidays the older children decorate the hall from floor to ceiling with large pictures painted on huge sheets of cheap paper. They choose a scheme and get down to it in the hall (where there is the most floor space) with brushes of all sizes and powdered water-colours. They also have life-classes on Thursday evenings, when the children and staff take it in turn to model, while a stop-watch ticks away: the idea is to get essentials down, and not become bogged down in detail. When there is a party, fancy dress dance, theatrical performance or bazaar, Harry has to be ready to help, if asked, by showing the children how best to carry out their often difficult ideas.

Art is not included in the time-table as a subject. Anyone is free to practise it if they want. The room is locked in the afternoon, when the day's lessons are over, but it is possible to make an arrangement with Harry, and you lock up again when you go. Compare this arrangement with that in Denmark, where art figures rigidly in the curriculum, twice a week from ten until twelve, it being expected that the children are at those fixed times in the mood to be creative.

There's no equipment that will suffer from hard treatment. The tables are old and battered, and so are the chairs. They are not much the worse for being spattered with wet clay. If a little paint is spilled, no one takes a cloth and turpentine and wipes it up. The art room is a play room, which is used preferably by the young ones who have not yet seen the expediency of going to lessons. What they make is little different from what is done in art rooms generally; but there is the important difference that no child is told what to do. It will be given guidance once it has embarked on something, if it wants it. If a child does come in and asks Harry what it should do, he turns it out, because why enter an art room if you don't know what you want to do? But no one is allowed to spoil things for the others in the art room, any more than elsewhere. The other day, I saw one little chap begin to amuse himself by flinging lumps of wet clay all over the place: the clay stuck to the walls, the roof, the floor. This of course violently irritated the other children, and the culprit was bundled out very quickly.

The children did not seem greatly interested in their

finished products. It was very rare for a child to sign a picture, and in their play with clay they were more interested in dramatizing the material. They built villages, harbours, tropical islands, airports, motorways, all done in a very facile way. They would then play with what they had made for a while, and when they tired of their game, they would squeeze the clay together again and start something new. But they did also make things for use or decoration. Money-boxes (so it was not only in the handicrafts room that wishful-thinking found concrete form), ashtrays, vases, and figures of people and animals were favourites. Most of these were given to the staff as presents.

I spent a lot of time in the art room, sometimes getting in the way, sometimes helping. It was one of the busiest places in the school, and so it was a pleasure to be there. The children would want colours mixing, or there was the big bucket of old greasy clay to be taken to the kitchen garden and emptied. And sometimes Lars would come and paint a picture or "ruin a piece of paper": the fact that he did sometimes paint a picture could perhaps be taken as a sign that there was improvement in him.

Today I began selecting pictures for an exhibition. The accumulated production was enormous. To avoid being buried in paper, every other year they burned what amounted to nine cubic metres of painted paper. As I sat rummaging in the heap, I remembered the journalist who on the occasion of Jens Søndergaard's seventieth birthday asked him what he was getting at with his pictures. Such a question is, of course, impossible to answer, but Søndergaard cleverly got out of it by saying: "Power of colour, damn it!" He was an artist in the professional sense, which children are not, and they would not be able to express in words anything about their pictures, most of which were expressions of the changing state of their minds—and for that very reason had a large element of "power of colour" in them.

* * *

An extraordinary meeting was held at eleven o'clock today. The atmosphere is always a bit charged before such meetings, because either something urgent and important is to be discussed, something that cannot wait until the Saturday meeting, or it concerns a matter which for one reason or another had best be kept from visitors. Today's business was the case of a fifteen-year-old girl, just come to Summerhill from the U.S., who had taken a boy from the International Club back to the school with her after school bedtime. This was a delicate matter that would have earned expulsion in Denmark from any boarding-school having pupils of her age. It was disposed of here in an atmosphere of orderly quiet: no agitated voices or heated argument, no moral indignation, no scandalized expressions. I was reminded of the case of a boy and a girl from the top form of a camp school in Denmark. A hysterical, frustrated mistress had discovered them lying petting and she had sent them home. (True, the progressive organs of the Danish press attacked the poor woman.) In the case we were dealing with here, one might have expected Neill to make some pronouncement before the assembly announced its finding, but he did not. For the fifteen minutes the meeting lasted, he just stood listening. But when the girl had been given a severe warning, and orders that she must not do anything like this again, Neill put up his hand and made the concluding remarks. He said: "This case has nothing to do with morals. You must realize that what you have done is, first and foremost, to contravene the accepted bedtime by coming back late from the town. The fact that you had a visitor with you is neither here nor there. But you must know that everyone here wants to be quite clear who is a visitor and who belongs here. That is a reasonable requirement, as we all have to live here. We have to know who comes home —even after nightfall."

Those remarks demonstrated that Neill was in full agreement with the attitude the assembly had adopted towards the case. There had not been a debate on sexual intercourse, but a debate on keeping the laws they had all helped to pass. That is not only courageous pedagogics, but also right—for those who dare.

Thursday, November 22

It is typical that the opponents of the school where instruction is absolutely free pounce on the cases of children leaving Summerhill at the age of fourteen or sixteen without having attended a single class. These cases, of course, are few and far between. I believe there have been only three, which ought to be proof enough that children wish to learn. The point on which the well-informed opponents of the idea seize is that the children are not invited by the staff to take part in the lessons. It is so ingrained in us that we have to be invited before we will do pretty well anything. Many schoolmasters will agree with me that teaching must contain a large element of invitation and persuasion before any progress can be made. This is especially true of the top forms. Even reasonable parents and semi-progressive pedagogues cannot help being infected by the poison of expediency when a wealth of tempting job offers beckon and so many obstacles have to be overcome. It is so understandable that it is almost forgivable. No matter how rooted one's belief in personal freedom, many people would feel that they were failing their children if they did not urge them along. I do not shut my eyes to this, but it is a ghastly mistake in education to make urging standard practice.

This morning I saw Ted in front of the noticeboard copying down the time-table for Form Five. He was going to classes now, but not at anybody's invitation. Before coming to Summerhill he had gone to a school in America, a school he could not stomach. He had been a year at Summerhill and all that time he had not attended a class. But now he felt he wanted to, because he knew what he wanted to be; and because the others had told him so much that was fun that they had learned there. Here of course the persuasive factor does enter—all right, but it is not persuasion from the side of authority. What his companions had done was merely to recommend a commodity. If it turned out that he was bored in class and got nothing out of lessons, he would be free to walk out at any time.

His keenness to attend lessons infected me. I also wondered how long a "holiday" from lessons I would have taken if I had been sent to Summerhill at his age. Ted was eleven when he came. I think I would have reacted very much as he had, because our two cases were similar in many ways. And I had been visiting Summerhill for a month now, and had not attended a lesson nor been invited to do so; but now suddenly I wanted to. It would be useless to pretend that I had not known there were lessons going on. It was, after all, a school I was visiting. But the extra-curricular activities were so many that they often stole the limelight. To put it another way: just as in the beginning I had found it difficult to distinguish staff from pupils, I still had difficulty in distinguishing lessons from free time. The school does not throb with life during breaks and lie quiet while lessons are in progress. It is lively all the time. Active instruction is not limited to the class periods. During breaks and in their so-called free time the children go to their teachers with questions, and they sit in their rooms or in the library and work. It often happened that when I was sitting with Harry in the afternoon, Fritz would come for a German lesson. The first time this happened, I got up to go, but Harry told me to sit where I was, because I would not bother him. So now Harry has not one but two pupils. I must admit, however, that I do not attend as regularly as Fritz.

Today, however, I felt that I wanted to see what went on behind the closed form-room doors. At the eleven o'clock break, just after I had been talking to Ted, I announced in the common room that now I wanted to attend lessons. They laughed at that and said that it was certainly high time, but which lessons did I wish to attend? They expected me to have a plan ready now that I had decided. Well, I wanted to have English with Jane, mathematics and science with Paul, and biology and Latin with Oliver. I wanted to be with the fourth form, which was where I thought I belonged. I was not interested in Neill's English lessons. His method of teaching is explained in detail in his books and what is not actually stated can be read between the lines. I was more interested in seeing how teachers of my own generation tackled their job.

All except Oliver were ready for me to come to their next lesson in the subjects I mentioned. Oliver did not want visitors attending his classes under any circumstances. He had had them a couple of times and on each occasion the children had been more interested in the visitors than in what was being taught. So that I must do without. Oliver, grinning conciliatingly, said that we could always have a beer together in the pub, and when it closed, go on to the fish and chip shop, as we had been doing these last couple of weeks. I thanked him deferentially, whereupon he hastened to remind me that it was my turn to pay for the fish and chips.

Only five had come for Jane's English lesson. The three girls knitted through most of the lesson, but that did not mean that they were not concentrating on the subject just as much as the boys, who weren't doing anything with their hands. The class had just done an essay and they were taking turns to read their efforts out, after which Jane and the others offered criticisms. Then Jane collected the essays to correct the spelling, and they began analysing a passage from the form book. They managed this excellently; I could not have done it much better myself. Once or twice I could not agree with Jane's instruction, but who was to decide which of us was right; both of us were teachers, and there was no arbitrator there.

Analysis calls for a certain degree of maturity to find it interesting. It is difficult to make analysis creative. What counts is dry fact and it is included in one's teaching out of consideration for those who are working for an exam. How much use linguistic analysis is to a future butcher's apprentice or an engineer does not concern us here. All one can say is that in order to achieve this or that, this and the other are required. Children are aware of many of our pedagogic absurdities and they accept them in order to achieve what interests them.

Paul's form was dealing with resistances and their symbols. The blackboard was filled with complicated equations and difficult fraction lines, and several of the pupils had to have it explained and worked through a couple of times extra (as one says: but extra to *what?*). It was an appreciable help to understanding when they began working out the resistances in a wireless receiver which a couple of boys coaxed into producing a little sound. Theory was applied to a concrete situation and that pays dividends, as any schoolmaster will tell you.

In Paul's science lesson they were revising density and specific heat, after which the form split into groups for independent experiment.

Understandably there is not much new under the sun or in these lessons, and it is questionable whether there is much new that could be put in. The fifth is the top form at Summerhill. Those pupils who wanted instruction had to submit to the requirement of learning facts by heart. Neill does not subscribe to Montessori's theories of teaching children through play. But that does not mean that play is banished from the form-room. Play can very easily find expression in humour and there is plenty of that at Summerhill. The Summerhill staff are naturally free to choose their own methods; Neill does not interfere with the way they teach. Thus one could well imagine someone who swore by the learn-through-play idea being on the staff, but I did not meet one. The fact that the youngest are played with both in the form-room and in their free time is, of course, an entirely different matter; this play is more for its own sake than for the purpose of teaching. At Summerhill they have made the exceptional discovery that childhood and play go together. May other schools soon do the same!

The system of forms and how the pupils are classified is very elastic at Summerhill. Forms are numbered from one to five, and children can be at the school from five, six, or seven until fourteen, fifteen or sixteen. Thus from the Danish point of view a couple of forms are missing; but at Summerhill it all works out because the numbers in the form are small and because no one worries about age and form having to correspond. In putting children in this form or that, it is more their degree of maturity and knowledge that count than age. Naturally, age is a factor, but it is not a decisive one. The quality of the teaching is such that children can go from the fifth form to senior school. This is not due solely to the staff, who are good, it is true, head and shoulders above the Danish average, but rather to the fact that the pupils attend because they want to. It goes without saying that work flows more easily then, and the pace of learning can be increased. At Summerhill there have been cases of children learning in one year what children in State schools take three or four years to learn.

The time-tables for the various forms are as follows:

Forms 1 and 2. 5 periods of arithmetic, 15 periods of English and creative work aimed at acquiring one's mother tongue, 5 periods of handicraft. Twenty-five periods in all for the week.

Form 3. 8 periods of handicrafts, 4 periods each of history, English, arithmetic, biology, French, 1 period of Latin and 6 periods of science. A total of thirty-five periods for the week.

Form 4. 4 periods each of history, arithmetic, French

English, biology, one period of Latin, 6 periods of science, and 8 periods of handicrafts. In all thirty-five periods in the week.

Form 5. 4 periods each of biology, history, French and handicrafts, 3 periods of English, 5 periods of arithmetic, 2 periods of independent work under guidance and 1 period of Latin. Altogether twenty-seven periods in the week.

The smaller number of periods for the fifth form allows those in it to do more individual work on the subjects in which they have to attain a certain standard in order to continue their education elsewhere, where the system is different.

The length of the periods varies:

first	9.30 —	10.10
second	10.10 —	10.50
third	11.10 —	11.50
fourth	11.50 —	12.30
fifth	12.30 —	13.10
sixth	16.30 —	17.30
seventh	17.30 —	18.00

There is a break of approximately five minutes between each period and the next, and these do not figure in the time-table. The staff assemble for tea between the second and third period, when the children have a glass of milk. Lunch and free time come between the fifth and sixth period. The sixth period acts as a sort of double period and, generally, the sixth and seventh periods are devoted to subjects on which it is possible to concentrate for longer periods or for which longer time is required; that is to say, principally manual skills.

The periods are thus mostly of 40 minutes, and on the average each period is further shortened by two and a half minutes for the break between lessons, making periods of 37½ minutes. This fits in well with the results of the experiments made into how long children can concentrate, namely between twenty-five and thirty-five minutes. So here, too, Summerhill sticks close to realities.

Thursday, November 24

Nine-year-old Neil came up to me today and showed me a letter from his mother. "Hurrah!" he said, "I'm going to Denmark for the summer holidays. That's where you live, isn't it?" And he jumped about round me while I read the letter. Yes, it was, I told him. And, true enough, Neil's mother was taking him to Denmark for the holidays. So, of course, he wanted to learn Danish, and that I could teach him, couldn't I? Neil did not go to any of the classes, but he was one of the most active in the art room, and so did not merit being labelled "lazy" because he could not be bothered with school subjects. I wanted to be sure that he meant what he said, and so I told him that I did not want to start today, but that we could tomorrow. I asked him to find out by tomorrow exactly what he wanted to learn to say in Danish. I thought that it would be good for him to have a little time in which to think things over, and for him to have something to look forward to. "When will you be coming tomorrow?" he asked. I promised to come in the forenoon.

Neil came bounding down the stairs several at a time as I entered the hall. He had seen me coming from his window. He was ready to start there and then, with us standing on either side of the horse, but after a little parleying we agreed to go up to his room. Neil shared a room with seven others, girls and boys, up on the top floor of the main building, where Lars also was. It was a big room, as it needed to be to take so many, but not so large that it looked like a dormitory. The children had seen to that. Things had been put up on almost every available space: on the walls colourful posters and drawings, and some of the ends of the bunks had been painted on. Festoons of shiny paper hung between the beds and some of the lower bunks were arranged as caves, with blankets hanging down from the bunk above. Although the room had been "done" some three hours earlier, the floor was littered with pieces and snippets of paper. Neil had one of the lower bunks and there he was able to have his first Danish lesson undisturbed. The very first thing he wanted to learn was the Danish for "I am hungry". I commended this for its practical use for a boy who can eat most of a packet of porridge oats for breakfast. Neil was quite quick to learn. Within five minutes he was able to say the three words so that they were understandable. I then asked him if there was anything more he wanted to say. He wanted to learn to count. I taught him up to five and he mastered this very quickly. He then wanted the next five to take him to ten. When he could count from five to ten, I asked him to join the two lots together, but then he got mixed up, though he could still remember the first sentence. This encouraged him, and now he wanted to learn to say "You are stupid," in order to be able to say it to Lars, who had so often said it to him—this was one of the few things Lars could say properly in English. Vengeance is sweet! Lars was to be repaid in his own coin. So I taught Neil to say what he wanted; who knows, it might start a friendship between them. And that's how it worked out. Neil learned the new sentence in no time at all; then he rushed off to Lars, shouting "Du er dum!" Lars came in grinning and asked me if I had been teaching Neil. He added: "Neil says it almost in Norwegian." I explained that this was due to the lilt almost all languages have except hard Danish. Lars seemed not in the least annoyed at being called stupid, which pleased me. They kept up a joint barrage of "You are stupid" for some time, each in his foreign language. The noise brought others in, and when it dawned on them that Neil was starting to learn Danish, they wanted to do so too. Neil now had to deal with competition. Soon lots of them, Lars included, could count to ten; as well as say: You are stupid. I am hungry. I then announced that the lesson was over for the day.

Monday, November 28

The first day of Neil's Danish lesson had been the greatest fun. After that he consolidated his progress by adding to his store of knowledge two more sentences: "When am I to go back home?" and "I am thirsty". When I asked him if there was anything more he wanted to know, he said that there wasn't. He knew enough now! He was more concerned with getting to the art room, where he was working on a paper costume for an impending fancy-dress party. And why learn more when you feel you can manage?

When I was going down to the hall, I saw that the bathroom was awash. Four children had filled the bath and were sailing ships that they had made in the handicrafts room. It looked as if they were afloat too. The commotion brought the house-mother and she stopped the worst of the flooding. Playing with water is forbidden indoors, so the four may find themselves on the agenda for the next Saturday meeting.

Perhaps the reader has received the impression that visitors are not welcome at Summerhill. If so, let me try to put that right. For visitors the first few days are the most difficult—as they are for the children. They have to sum people up. The visitor is tipped into a world which, though he has certainly heard about, he probably has not been able to envisage. The Summerhill children like best those visitors who in one way or another can amuse or entertain them. The week before I got there, Joan Baez, the protester, had been at the school. One evening she had sung and played to the whole school and had had a tremendous success. They were still talking about it. Obviously, not many people are able to spellbind an audience of children with a performance of any kind, but there are other ways. A visitor who can—and will—play with the children is usually sure of a welcome. This, of course, applies mainly to younger ones, but it is interesting that a visitor who finds acceptance with the small fry is automatically accepted by the older ones as well. There is a sense of solidarity and a protective tendency at the school. This does not strike one immediately; it is something which one becomes aware of gradually.

Never at any time have I felt *unwelcome* here, but it would be wrong to say that I felt *welcome* from the start. The children's attitude seemed at first to be one of indifference, and perhaps I did not feel unwelcome then, because I had so thoroughly prepared myself for my visit. I was not able to catch the children's interest at once. I cannot do conjuring tricks or walk the tightrope, nor am I a ventriloquist. But I can "cut my throat", "tear off my thumb", and do other trifles that amuse children. It is natural for children to play. We grown-ups understand that with our minds, but not with our hearts, and what the mind comprehends is very limited. Thus it is healthy for adults to play—even just now and again—so as to revive the child in themselves.

The school had a visit from a "funny man" today. He was an American from San Francisco, an entertainer and conjurer. He made things disappear and pop up again. And not just small things. He juggled with boxes and bottles, and the children were wildly enthusiastic. Sometimes the tension was almost unbearable. Some of the tinies tried to see what he had hidden in his sleeves, or under the table. Neill had to call these inquisitives to order and tell them to sit down.

Neill was so delighted by the man and his performance that he invited him across to his house and regaled him with whisky. Today I have been with the magician to show him where to buy spirits, as he wanted to make Neill a present of a bottle of his favourite brand, and his powers, unfortunately, did not extend to magicking it.

Wednesday, November 30

Latterly Lars has become accustomed to my speaking to him more and more in English. This, of course, is partly because he is understanding more of the language. He is now playing with the others more, and so he has to use the language, but to him the other children are still "peculiar", "silly" and "very sexy", the last being the worst thing he can say about them.

Yesterday he met with a defeat. He had invited me up to his room. I noticed that his feet were trailing as he mounted the last few stairs, and as we stood outside the door of his room he regretted his invitation. "The others are in there," he said. Well, what about it? He had invited me, so it could not matter if they were. But it did. "The others don't want me to invite anyone." "Have they said so?" I asked. He did not answer that, but he said: "I'm afraid!" "All right," I said, "if you're afraid, we'll go down again." And that's what we did.

I couldn't make out whether he had talked with his roommates about it afterwards, but today he repeated his invitation. And went through with it.

His three room-mates were sitting on their beds as we entered. I knew them well and was on the best terms with them. They smiled and said good morning. Naturally I was not expecting to be chucked out, and it was a bit of a mystery to me why Lars should be so afraid of them. Possibly he had spoken so much against them to me and to himself that he had ended by expecting their hostility; or perhaps fear of law-breaking was still so deeply rooted in his mind that he had seen himself being reported at a meeting; or perhaps a mixture of both—or something else altogether.

But he seemed not in any way uneasy while we sat talking. Once or twice, when I translated a sentence, he said: "I understand that."

Thursday, December 1

Breakfast at the hotel is between half past eight and half past nine. At nine o'clock I grope my way to my table by the window and sleep on over the front page of the *Daily Telegraph* until my grapefruit is set before me. For a long time I have had the table to myself. At times I have had the whole dining-room, the entire hotel, to myself. Leiston is as small as that. The last two days, however, I have had the company of an estate agent. I am very taciturn in the morning, so I have left it to him to start any conversation. Two mornings running he has bidden me a loud, jovial Good Morning. Even such a salute can be extraordinarily irritating. And it soon transpires that there was more to come. He is at Leiston on business, and he expects me to talk about the place.

He had once heard something about Summerhill; was it really in Leiston? Naturally I was interested in what he had heard about Summerhill. Well, he had heard that it was a school where children were allowed to do as they liked and where boys and girls slept together and used the bathroom together. Was that right? His eyes were wide and avid for sensation. Alas, I had to disabuse him. It was true that girls and boys did share rooms, but only the young ones and only those who wished to. The older ones, I said, had to observe the ways of our antediluvian society, etc. He nodded. But sharing a bathroom?—what mightn't happen there? I admitted that all sorts of strange things might happen, but pointed out that so far nothing "serious" had happened, because if it had the school would have been shut down. Yes, true enough, for that was the law. I asked him if he did not think the law idiotic. He did not. So I shifted the conversation to a more personal plane, and asked him if he could see himself sending his children to Summerhill. He could not. Not in his wildest dreams! He was sure they wouldn't learn

much there. I bombarded him with examples of how well it all worked.

He sat for a while gazing out of the window. Outside, in Waterloo Avenue, a "sweater girl" was coming towards the hotel, as she did every morning at about this time. I would be a liar if I pretended I had not noticed her before. As she passed the window the estate agent turned to me and said: "There's something for you. What breasts!"

Indeed—what breasts!

At one of the Saturday meetings one of the visitors asked if Neill would go to the U.S.A.; if so, he would arrange a lecture-tour for him. Neill replied that he was now too old to undertake so long a trip, and had curtailed his lecturing activities considerably, though he still gave the odd lecture at places not too far from Summerhill. And now at his advanced age he had started doing what he had never done before: he travelled first-class. First-class carriages were half empty and you weren't so crushed.

Today Neill had gone off to a seminar somewhere to explain his revolutionary ideas. I came across Carla, from his English class, standing outside the main building looking perplexed. She volunteered the opinion that everything was so boring when Neill was not at the school. "Now we'll miss English both today and tomorrow. Lessons with him are such fun," she said. I asked if the others in the class shared her opinion and she was quite definite that they did. I could not help thinking of my own schooldays and the noisy delight that greeted the announcement that one of the masters was not coming, only dampened if a substitute had been found; and him we would then seek to provoke to some shaming outburst of rage. I remembered our vile joy when the German master fell off his chair and landed with a bump on his tail.

There is about seventy years difference in age between Neill and his pupils. I am sure that much of the boredom in schools is due to the difference in age between master and pupil, and to the enormous intellectual gap between them. Teachers are so often elderly, and wearied by life, and cannot get on to the wavelength of the young. But the years are strange things: they do not always abide by the rules. Masters much younger than Neill appear senile by comparison. Neill is a good teacher because he does not stand on his dignity, is not pompous, and has faith in children. He believes that in their hearts they are good, that they want to learn, and that they can be happy. So many schoolmasters feel insulted and lose their tempers if a child calls them an "old idiot", or puts out its tongue, or says "shut up". The "good teacher" will remain something of a myth for as long as teachers have themselves to go through the old educational mill. But the reaction will have to come. Change is seeping through here and there. Whether Summerhill conditions could ever become general is, indeed, questionable; indeed it is arguable that Summerhill on a wider scale would only mean another form of indoctrination. What is it I want, then? I want man to be free, by one means or another, because I subordinate society to the individual.

Monday, December 5

A student of psychology at Belfast University arrived here on a visit last Saturday. At the Saturday meeting Neill asked him if he was learning psychology by studying the behaviour of rats. Yes, he was. They both laughed.

A year or two ago this chap from Belfast had a grant to go to China, and he brought two hundred slides to Summerhill with him. Would we like to see them? We would indeed. It was realized that they would appeal more to the staff and older children, but the younger children were still allowed in for the lecture, which he gave yesterday evening. In the afternoon he and I went through the slides to select those that would say something to the tinies as well. When we had chosen the fifty with the greatest epic content, the Belfast man told me that he was a bit nervous. He had never lectured to so young an audience: wouldn't the tinies kick up an awful row? He thought the young ones would be bored. I didn't. But I advised him to raise his voice and drown any noise they made. And if it got too much, he must just turn them out. This was his evening, after all.

The slides were shown in the theatre, which is perhaps twenty-five feet by ten feet. The first three rows have proper tip-up theatre seats. The smallest are put in the front rows, and so on according to height. The first few rows were in high spirits even before the performance began, bouncing on their seats and letting them clap back as a foretaste of the applause the pictures would get. Neill was not present. He, I am sure, had seen enough slides in his life and preferred conjuring tricks and magic. Eventually the projector was set up, the lights turned out, and the first slide appeared on the screen. The small fry endured the first ten or eleven pictures, then some of them got up on to the stage and disappeared behind the screen. Others followed. Up there they performed their own play: clambering about the props, making noises, calling out, fighting, tumbling about, moving tables and chairs. The bigger ones, who wanted to watch the slides, protested violently and that helped for a bit. But then one of the most active of the tinies did a Tarzan act across the front of the screen, and that was too much for Oliver. He cleared the presumptuous tinies out of their cave and turned the worst disturbers out. Others went of their own accord. The lecturer took it all very calmly, in fact, he was able to laugh at it. After that, there was only shuffling and small disturbances, and when we came to the most dramatic pictures, the Great Wall seen from various angles, there was utter silence. The Great Wall is some 2,700 miles long and it took only ten years to build. Obviously mostly slave-labour was used to build it; otherwise it would never have been finished. Many died of their exertions and their bodies were immediately cemented into the wall. The Great Wall is thus the world's largest cemetery. It is also the only man-made object that can be seen from the moon. This was stuff that commanded silence. Once this excitement was over, the rest of the young ones left the theatre, all except Marc. Marc is six. When the last slide had been shown, some of the bigger children went up to the lecturer with questions. Marc also went up. "Lot of silly pictures you showed us!" he said.

We had to go outside and laugh.

Tuesday, December 6

Lars has not started going to lessons yet. It would have surprised me greatly if he had. I am sure that if he had, it would not be out of conviction or interest, but as the result either of an injunction from home or of his own bad conscience. With almost every day that passes he is being accepted by more of his fellows and he is not accusing them or complaining about them nearly as much as he did. He now plays for hours on end and speaks English a lot. He is no longer there to greet me when I arrive. Nor does he ask now if I am coming in the morning, but that perhaps is because he has discovered that I do in fact come every day. He is more active in the art room and he is trying to free himself from stupid convention by wearing a hat; he is always wearing his optimist-green cap. "Take that hat off indoors," I said to him yesterday. He laughed and told me I was silly. He seldom expresses himself as freely and frankly.

Today I went into the library. Lars must have seen me go in, because he followed almost at once. He never enters the place unless he is with someone. "You mustn't be in here," he told me now. "You haven't been invited." "You're perfectly right. At the moment I am breaking one of your laws and I'm ready to pay a sixpenny fine, but you will have to bring it up at the meeting in English!—otherwise you won't be understood, and there's a limit to what I'll translate for you." Lars began to backpedal: what I was doing wasn't so awful, and I had been at the school so long now, nobody would mind, he thought. Then he said something I could scarcely credit: "I've something else I want to bring up at the meeting." I managed to conceal my surprise, and nodded encouragingly. I did not even question him; I decided to restrain my curiosity until Saturday. Lars presumably was feeling on top of things, and wanted to exploit the situation.

Wednesday, December, 7

For the last week I have been working a couple of hours a day in the theatre, to which Harry has given me his key. The quantity of pictures to be sorted through is so huge that it is more sensible to work in a large space, and undisturbed. Here, also, I can mend the worst tears and holes before sending the pictures off to Denmark. When I arrived today to finish sorting and to put them together for despatch tomorrow, I saw that the door was not locked; there were people inside, up on the stage. I hesitated about going in, but as I felt I had a certain right to the place, in I went. No one asked me to leave, which I had half expected for I knew that the children disliked visitors witnessing their rehearsals. I was even given a seat in the front row.

The actors were all girls aged between nine and eleven. I had heard and read a lot about the freedom of their acting and this was very true. The producer, who acted with them, tended to overlook exaggerated movements. For example, when a girl had to faint in an armchair with its back to the auditorium, the last one saw of her was her hands flapping above the back of the chair. She kept moving them for so long, she might have been waving goodbye to someone in a

SUMMERHILL DIARY

slow train The actors had a clear, unnervous diction, and what they said could be plainly heard. I wondered whether this was because no grown-up had anything to do with the play. Anyone who has produced a children's play knows what a labour it is to get the cast to speak up so that the audience can hear. Really, it is only those with inherent talent for acting who make any sort of show at the early rehearsals, and it was obvious that not all on the stage had the same sense of theatre as the producer; but they were at no time afraid of letting their voices be heard. They acted with a keenness I cannot remember having seen in adult amateurs. They accepted all the producer's corrections without grumbling, though they did question and discuss, and subsequently ask if that had been good enough. They combined mimicry with feeling. They understood the words and felt them as if they were reality; their bodies were relaxed and their thoughts concentrated on their acting. The play was about a bourgeois wife with no other interests than her telephone and her court of maid-servants. The whole thing lasted half an hour. The children had written it themselves and its first performance was to be on the 19th, at the end of term. They had no props and these were indeed unnecessary, as the telephone, vacuum cleaner, brooms and so on, were so well suggested that they were *there*. This particularly impressed me. How often with school productions does the property master have to work overtime because the actors can't manage without a whole lot of tangible details. There are not many children who can kick at a stone unless there is one lying on the stage, and there always has to be an artificial noise from the wings. During the rehearsal I was not aware of any technicalities off stage. Those who were not acting remained quiet at the back. At the end I asked one of the girls if they really did everything themselves without help of the staff. They did. But it might happen, if they were short of a play, that Neill or Harry or another member of the staff would write one for them. The one I had just seen, however, was all their own work.

A great deal is written about crisis in the theatre and the young generation's lack of interest in this branch of art. But if there really is a crisis, may it not conceivably be partly the fault of the schools? How many schools allow the pupils to decide what they shall act? How many plays are written by the pupils themselves? Why do so many schools demand quality instead of allowing experimental self-activity? Why are so many adults afraid of children's inability to tell chalk from cheese?

Thursday, December 8

Those who have visited Summerhill hold every conceivable shade of opinion about it. Some arrive prejudiced in its favour, others come prejudiced against it; and often what they see just confirms their views. But it can happen that first-hand experience of the place can cause their views to change radically. There was an example of this the other day. A Norwegian visitor arrived. He had heard and read a lot about the school and was very much in favour of it. However, as luck would have it the youngest child at the school, a five-year-old orphan from America, directed all his undeclared, emotional love on to this Norwegian, who found such behaviour odd and regarded it as a bad sign. Because he was an orphan and because the director of an orphan home in the U.S.A. knew Neill, Paul had been accepted against Summerhill rules about minimum age, which are broken now and then. Paul is far from being a problem child. He has lots of charm, is active and energetic, quite a little bombshell in fact, and in all this no different from many others of his age. The Norwegian was not his first substitute father. When so many of the others had visitors on Saturdays, why shouldn't Paul think up a father? There was nothing unnatural in that, and it was what he used to do. If his "father" was accompanied by a woman, she obviously became his "mother". I had witnessed this little comedy several times, and the new "parents" (usually different ones each Saturday) always played up, as did their own children. Paul was well-liked by all, especially by the older girls, whose pet he was. I believe he enjoyed having so many parents, as none of the others had. When I had been there only three or four days, Paul told me I was his father, to which I at once agreed. At that time I did not know his background, but assumed that there was a reason why I should so suddenly be made his father. We have played together. I have been with him in San, where his room is, and at the Saturday meetings he has sometimes snuggled up to me, to be taken on my lap. But he has never hung round me as Lars did at the beginning of our acquaintance, and when he did not want my company any more, he would just walk off, feeling perfectly free to go and without explanation of or excuse for where he was going. He plays a lot with Kenny, who is only a year older, and on several occasions I have been caught between their shields and promised a sound drubbing with their swords if I would not go voluntarily to their HQ as their prisoner. I got a lot of enjoyment out of my friendship with Paul and I have not observed the least sign of his being distressed at being at Summerhill.

But the Norwegian was of a different opinion. Paul, he thought, did not feel at home at Summerhill. Moreover, he was too young to be there, and no one there paid proper attention to him. I did not agree with any of this. The Norwegian spent four days at the school. On the last day, we were sitting on the stairs in the main building discussing Paul, who was crawling round us playing. We each spoke in our own mother tongue and, of course, Paul did not understand a word of our talk. But he tumbled to it that we were talking about him, even though we had not once spoken his name. At least I cannot think of any other possible explanation of his behaviour. All at once he put his mouth to my ear and yelled, effectively jamming communications. I took him on my knee, and said to the Norwegian that we must change the subject. "Yes, indeed," the Norwegian said. "There you are. There are problems with the boy." No sooner had he said that than Paul began yelling again, this time into the Norwegian's ear. Paul was demonstrating with convincing force that children sense more than we adults like. Anyway, we now changed the subject, without having reached agreement, and soon the hostile glint disappeared from Paul's eyes.

Then one of the older girls came up and asked Paul if he would like to dance, and the two of them went off swinging across the floor. We were now able to continue our interrupted discussion, for Paul was absorbed in the dance, whirling a couple of inches over the floor as the girl swung him round. I maintained that Paul's yells were merely the result of his having realized that we were talking about him; while the Norwegian continued to insist that Paul would be best off in the company of those of his own age and that his yells were evidence of this. The Norwegian was the director of a home for children of just Paul's age, four to six. Like so many of us, he was trying to build conclusions on the basis of experiences that had become dogma.

Today Paul asked me if I would go with him to San while he had supper. His house-mother was called Sheila. She was nineteen, but so like the best type of mother that one might have thought all twelve children were her own. The children have supper in their own sections at five o'clock. Sheila brought trays of bread and butter, cold meat and milk from the kitchens in the main building; then the children queued up in front of the sideboard and were given a plate of things they themselves chose. Table manners were non-existent. Free children make plenty of noise while they are eating, but I can endorse the fact that unfree children make even more noise if they get the chance. A great deal of bartering went on at the low tables, with much parleying. As soon as a child had finished, it just stood up and walked away: no question of all trooping out together. One or two handed their empty plates to Sheila, but no one was rebuked for leaving his on the table. Only one or two of the oldest in San used a knife or fork. Most of them thrust the food into their mouths with their fingers and pressed it home with their thumbs. If they tried to push in more roast beef than would go, they tore off the protruding end and ate it with the next mouthful. There was a continual clatter of mugs and plates while they were eating, and conversation was not confined to their own tables. There was nothing peculiar in their behaviour, nor unappetizing, for these were children. If you saw adults eating in this way, you would be taken aback, but upbringing must recognize the differences and similarities in children and adults, and this means, for one thing that one must not attach importance to non-essentials. Former Summerhill pupils are reputed to eat "normally" and "decently" in adult life.

Paul chattered away whether his mouth was stuffed or empty. He must have asked for too much, for at one point he pushed his plate across to me and asked me to finish it up. This was done secretively. I obliged.

As we were leaving San, Paul asked me when I was going back to Denmark, and when he heard that I was leaving on Sunday evening, he wanted to kiss me goodbye there and then, so as to be sure of having done so in case he did not see me again. If the Norwegian had been there still, our argument would have begun all over again. He would have told me that Paul had grown dependent on me; I do not believe that. Paul was a sensible boy and he made no secret of his feelings. Five minutes after kissing me goodbye, he would be running off to someone else to pick him up, and five minutes after I left Summerhill he would probably have forgotten me. And that is how it ought to be.

Saturday, December 10

The school's jazz band was at full blast when I arrived this afternoon. I went to the staff common room and sat and listened. The children were not playing from music, but were regarding their playing as spontaneous creativity, in line with their activities under Harry. They were improvising on blues themes. The band consisted of three ordinary guitars, one clarinet played by a former pupil, a trombone played by one of the house-mothers, and a lot of percussion handled mightily by a big boy whose torso swayed gently but whose arms and legs were moving so fast he did not appear to have any. They all jumped in their seats in time with the rhythm.

All at once Lars darted in and took up a position behind my chair. I could tell that there was something he wanted of me, but I pretended not to realize this, in order to leave the initiative to him. He knelt down beside the arm of my chair and told me that he had on him a big knife, which was forbidden for him as he was not old enough. "Would you like to see it?" he asked. I said I would, and I was pleased that he did not exact a promise about not telling anyone else about the knife. This meant that he regarded me as being on his side, which could be an indication that his authority-obsession was breaking down. What a pity I was having to leave, for it would have been no small gain for Lars' future here if his possession of the knife could have been publicised, so that he would have discovered that the assembly would not have punished him, as he expected, but have contented itself with issuing a warning and appealing to him not to carry the knife, which is all that would have happened. Now, from the depths of a pocket, he produced the knife, an ugly throwing knife with a long, broad blade, and he told me in a whispered, rather horrified voice that it was able to kill a person. It's quite something, in our world of strip cartoons and cheap thrillers, for a boy to feel he possesses a knife capable of killing. In my time I too have sworn by such knives, so I did not devalue its potentialities by telling him that murders have been committed with a nail file. I agreed that it was splendid and tested the sharpness of the blade with my thumb, in the manner of an expert. Indeed, it was a splendid weapon!

Latterly Ena had been wondering more and more whether Lars would come back after the Christmas holidays. Although some progress had been made in his relationship with the school and his association with the other children, and though he was gradually becoming quite good at simple English, he was not altogether happy to be there nor did he feel secure. If he had, he would certainly not have gone about with that knife. Lars, indeed, was counting the days, and soon it would be the hours, until the holidays began: I had the job of working it out for him. There was no doubt from the way he longed for home that he came from one where he was not free, but was developing under compulsion. It may sound paradoxical, but nonetheless it is the case that the problem children at Summerhill long to get back home. They weep violently when their parents say goodbye at the end of a visit. Things were particularly hard for the little boy who recently peed on the steps. His father had frequently smacked him and sometimes had even laid hands on his mother. One theory here is that the boy wants to get home in order to try to defend his mother; that may not be true, but it could be so. I have made the same discovery among young people of between fourteen and eighteen. The homesickness of those who came from an insecure home was in almost exact proportion to the degree of badness of their homes; while those who came from a balanced home were either not homesick at all or only fleetingly.

Lars surprised everyone at this evening's meeting. He kept his word and did what he had told me he would, the other evening in the library, when he said that he was going to speak in English at the next meeting. The words came stutteringly and their order was rather un-English, but they did come and they were understood. He was not accusing me. He was announcing the loss of his green cap. One of the boys said he had it. He had just "borrowed" it. Lars was asked if he wished the matter to be taken further and the borrower fined, but he did not.

At this meeting, as always someone asked questions about sex in the school. This evening Neill produced a viewpoint that corresponds with and throws light on my conversation with the estate agent at my hotel.

"Why hasn't there been a single case of pregnancy among the girls at the school?"

"I think this is largely because I explain to the older children what the consequences to the school would be if there was a case. But one must not forget that here there is no such problem as in other schools where boys and girls are together. Here they are accustomed from an early age to associate as brothers and sisters. One could also say, putting it briefly, that upbringing ought to make the unconscious conscious, while it seems to me that so-called normal upbringing strives to achieve the opposite, to make the conscious unconscious. Children must be assumed to be born with sexual consciousness. Sucking satisfies a sexual need in the infant as well as satisfying its hunger. The most important sense-organs of small children are the tongue and lips, and these organs function sensually, in the common meaning of the word. When a child becomes older it plays its sexual play and masturbates, which is quite natural—indeed it would be unnatural if a child didn't. But what usually happens? All their conscious sexuality is made unconscious by forbidding masturbation, by forbidding sexual play, by making sure the child's hands are outside the covers when it is put to bed, and by adults and parents often refusing information on sexual matters. And one could mention other examples of a child's conscious life being suppressed and undernourished. All this we try to avoid at this school and it would appear that we have succeeded quite well, because we talk with the children easily on sexual subjects, and because we do not check their sexual development when they are small. When they are older, we can only appeal to them, and so far that has worked."

Every excuse for a celebration is seized upon. This has been my last day at Summerhill on this visit, and though we meet at the pub every evening, this evening was a farewell occasion. "You must stand us all a beer," Oliver said, who looks like Henry VIII. After the third beer he said: "Tomorrow, when you've gone, we shall hoist the flag—we'll make one for the occasion." Harry thought I would soon be back, and Margaret said: "Now you'll go home and write a report for the Ministry of Education—do you think that will help?" But even in England people must know that it is the drops that wear away the stone.

Sunday, December 11

After I had spent a month at Leiston the shopkeepers began wondering why I was staying so long and they asked where I came from and what I was doing. When I told them that I was pottering about Summerhill seeing what went on there, some praised it: the children were always polite and natural, while Neill's reputation was high. No one spoke disparagingly of the place, though some just said: "Well!" Several, of course, were amazed that the school had been able to carry on so long. The manager of my hotel had this to say:

"Former Summerhill pupils often stay here when they come back to visit the school. They are friendly and polite. They arrive in their good clothes, but before they go to the school, they change into old things. Some years ago, a wedding reception for two former Summerhill pupils was held here. Among the guests were other former Summerhill pupils. Spirits became elevated during the evening, and unfortunately there was some quarrelling. Remarkably, none of the former Summerhill pupils took part in the quarrelling. They amused themselves splendidly all the evening. That may sound extraordinary, but so it was. My wife and I were very surprised."

He spoke a little about the strangely normal pupils of the school. I told him that putting on old clothes was a practical measure, as the younger children liked romping with visitors. On the whole, dress is not a thing taken very seriously at Summerhill. Harry and I talked about it one afternoon. I told him that in Denmark most children would not believe they were being taught by a schoolmaster, if one came from Summerhill, and that some school inspectors would request them to dress more suitably. Student-teachers at some colleges are told that a jacket should be buttoned up when writing on the blackboard; why, I have never discovered, but perhaps that is because I have never asked. Harry added that in the ordinary school a master who was not "well-dressed" would not be respected by the pupils. I was reminded of Antoine de Saint Exupéry's book *The Little Prince*, in which a Turkish astronomer goes to a congress and relates his discovery of a new planet. He is wearing Turkish dress and he is not believed. Some years later he goes to another such congress and relates exactly the same discovery. This time he is in Western European dress and is believed.

What is, perhaps, most characteristic of Summerhill is that there commitment is put before duty. Commitment is bound by inclination, duty by compulsion. It is impossible to imagine anyone teaching at Summerhill who did not want to be there. The small salary is the best proof of that. In the upbringing and instruction of the children, the staff undertake to allow them to be free and to want this freedom for others. This promotes tolerance. Neill is always asserting that Summerhill could not produce a Hitler, a fanatic about race, or a soldier who fought unthinkingly. The school has universal justification, but one of the most positive arguments for it is the fact that authority has made people into beings who do not know the motives for their actions, of which the total madness of total war is sufficient proof.

That may sound as if I regard Summerhill as something ideal. But what is ideal? I prefer the expression "suitable for its purpose". Summerhill is not an ideal place, but it is better than other schools. There is not much theorizing done at the school. Its results lie in the practical work which has proved its viability for more than forty years. There is thus no question of this being a pedagogic fashion. Without trying to say what the ideal would be, one can point to what is not ideal here: the atmosphere in the school was unable to rid Lars entirely of his fear of the meetings and so left him with his fear of the laws. It is a fact that some of the bigger boys sometimes bully smaller ones, and sometimes this is a problem which is very difficult to deal with without introducing the element of fear of authority. Here it is a question of a fine touch and feeling one's way. But I have the impression that any comparison of bullying at Summerhill and bullying in Danish schools would favour Summerhill, where there is so much else that is positive which the ordinary Danish school does not have.

What about the locked doors? Are those necessary in a free school? A good many visitors have wondered about this. Here, however, it is not just a question of prohibition for its own sake, as one often finds elsewhere. It is a question of reasons why, and there are plenty of these. For example, the theatre is kept locked. At one of the meetings I asked why this was done and was told that it was locked because a majority had asked that it should be, after some of the small fry had gone in one day and wrought havoc there. Sets had been ruined and the curtain torn to shreds. The art room was locked when the master was not there. For despite organized lack of order one could not allow chaos. The common room was the staff's and no one else's, except on Saturday afternoons when it was given over to music-making, because there is not a better or better-situated room. The younger children were not welcome in the common room, obviously, unless they came in search of one of the staff. They had spoiled too many chances. The children had their own domains, their interests, their inviolability, but so had the grown-ups, and it is this they succeed so amazingly well in teaching the children at Summerhill. The day that Summerhill's curve reaches the top again, there will be no reason to lock doors.

One may ask oneself whether this kind of school could be instituted on any large scale. The answer is definitely and regrettably—no! No system, whether in religion, politics, social structure or teaching, has proved to be perfect. It is not the system that counts, but the individual. Truth always becomes shaky when you try to organize it.

Neill says that Summerhill will be carried on in the same spirit after his death. I am not going to dispute that, for I am convinced that it will be so. But it will never be *quite* the same. The school will still be good (enough) and better than most, but the source of the initiative and the experience and knowledge will not be there. Others can and will run good schools, but no one can exactly copy Summerhill.

Neill ends one of his books with a story of how a young devil one day came running in great agitation to the Master and said: "Master, Master, something dreadful has happened. On earth they've discovered the truth!" The Devil smiled: "That's quite all right, Comrade. I'll send a group to organize it."

This book, too, ought to end with that.

102729

Segefjord, Bjarne.
Summerhill diary.